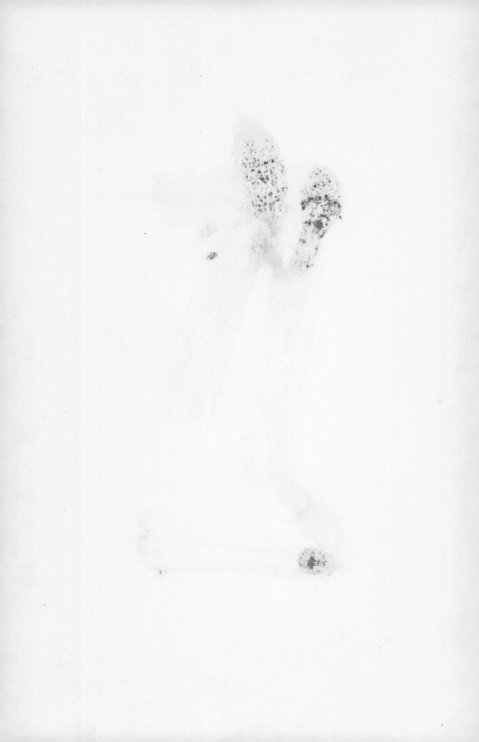

WHAT IS THE INCARNATION?

IS VOLUME

24

OF THE

Twentieth Century Encyclopedia of Catholicism

UNDER SECTION

II

THE BASIC TRUTHS

IT IS ALSO THE

90TH

VOLUME IN ORDER OF PUBLICATION

Edited by HENRI DANIEL-ROPS of the Académie Française

WHAT IS THE INCARNATION?

By *FRANCIS FERRIER*

Translated from the French by EDWARD SILLEM

HAWTHORN BOOKS · PUBLISHERS · New York

First Edition, July, 1962

NIHIL OBSTAT

Daniel Duivesteijn, S.T.D.

Censor Deputatus

IMPRIMATUR

E. Morrogh Bernard

Vicarius Generalis

Westmonasterii, die XVI APRILIS, MCMLXII

CONTENTS

INTRODUCTION

The Christian religion is unique among all the religions of the world in that its founder, Jesus of Nazareth, was not only a man like the founders of other religions, but also the very God who created and rules over all men and the universe in which they live. Jesus Christ is not merely the founder of the Christian religion; he is himself the focal point of everything comprised within it. He makes it to be the religion it is; without him nothing else would remain. For the Catholic, who believes that the Catholic Church is the one true Church of Christ on earth, Jesus Christ lives in the Church just as really as he used to live in Galilee and Judea. As Christ taught his disciples to know, love and serve him, so the work of the Church is to teach men to know, love and serve Christ. If the Church does that, she does everything; any Church which calls itself Christian must at least attempt to do that to justify its existence as a Christian community. In Christ the Christian has all he can possibly need for the life of his soul, and nothing else is of any value unless it somehow is connected with, or leads to Christ himself. Hence St Paul could write quite literally and truthfully to the Corinthians: "I had no thought of bringing you any other knowledge than that of Jesus Christ and of him as crucified" (1 Cor. 2. 2), and as regards himself he could say in all sincerity: "All this, which once stood to my credit, I now write down as loss, for the love of Christ. For that matter, there is nothing I do not write down as loss compared with the high privilege of knowing Christ Jesus, my Lord; for the love of him I have lost everything, treat everything else as refuse, if I may have Christ to my credit" (Phil. 3. 7–8).

How is Christ himself the very substance of Christianity, and of Catholicism in particular? In two ways. Firstly, in Christ we have the perfect human expression of God himself. Christ is God's own revelation of himself to us in living human form. The only adequate way in which we can all learn to know and love God is to know and love Jesus Christ. Christ is thus "the way" for all men to God himself, for it is in Christ that the Father takes us to himself. Thus St Paul writes: "The same God who bade light shine out of darkness has kindled a light in our hearts, whose shining is to make known his glory as he revealed it in the features of Jesus Christ" (2 Cor. 4. 6).

Secondly, Christ is the perfect expression of the "new creature" God plans to make of fallen man. Christ is the second Adam, the new man, the first-born of many brethren. Those who are baptized and believe in Christ become "new creatures", recreated in their being and in their minds. Thus St Paul reminded the Romans of what God demands of a Christian convert: "And you must not fall in with the manners of this world, there must be an inward change, a remaking of your minds, so that you can satisfy yourselves what is God's will, the good thing, the desirable thing, the perfect thing" (Rom. 12. 2).

It would scarcely be possible to exaggerate the importance of the theology of the Incarnation for anyone who prides himself on being a Christian, and there can scarcely be any subject in theology the study of which can be more fruitful and more rewarding. We think much about someone we know and love. How, then, are we to think about Jesus Christ? The obvious way to answer this question is to ask another: How does the Church herself think of the Christ who lives in her midst and whom she preaches to all men? Mere thinking about Christ will not, of course, lead a man to believe in him, nor to love him. But thinking about Christ in whom we do believe and whom we do love is one way of bringing Christ more and more into our lives and thus enlivening our faith in him. The more we try, in union with the Church, to think about Christ, the more we try to keep him in our minds by quiet reflection, the more we shall be living with him, and the better we shall come to realize that in him "the whole treasury of wisdom and knowledge is stored up" (Col. 2. 3). Doubtless, we all believe exactly what St Paul believed about Christ: but how different are our ways of thinking about him from St Paul's! St Paul challenges our all too human thoughts about Christ. He just states quite spontaneously how he thinks about the Christ he knows and loves: we believe sincerely in the truth of what he says, but how difficult it is to say that his way of thinking about Christ comes easily to us!

This book is not concerned with the life of Christ. It is concerned with Christ himself as he is known to Catholic dogma and theology. The Christ of theory is, of course, the Christ of history whom the apostles and evangelists know. But throughout the 2,000 years of the Church's history theologians have thought about Christ with the aid of a metaphysics and a language which the Church has made her own, and which all the Church's theologians share in common. We learn this language from the Church and her theologians, and we in our turn teach it to others. Anyone who seriously intends to associate himself with this great body of Christian theologians in order to learn from them what he can about Christ, must, of course, be prepared to learn their language and to think in their well-tried idiom before he can even hope to be able to appreciate what they have to teach him. The reader of this little book will learn something about this language and the extraordinary history of its origins. The language is really that of the Church herself: she teaches us, for example, that because "The Word was made flesh" we must venerate the hypostatic union of two natures in the eternal Person of the Word of God the Father. It may be that this sacred language is unknown to the modern secular world which knows not Christ; the fact is, however, that this language is, and always has been, the language loved and treasured by Catholics, and all orthodox Christians of all nations and tongues, and one which the experience of centuries has proved to be the best suited to the deepest intellectual and religious needs of men in meditating on Christ who transcends the limitations of any one age or tongue, like those of space and time itself. "What Jesus Christ was yesterday, and is today, he remains for ever" (Heb. 13. 8). This language is not beyond the layman who is prepared to make the necessary efforts to master it (the rewards for his labours will more than compensate him for his efforts), and it is as much a living language today as the Church is a living society.

There is no end to the theology of the Incarnation: it enters into every conceivable part of theology. This little book just asks one question: What is the Incarnation? What is the mystery of Jesus, Son of God and Son of man? What is the hypostatic union?

CHAPTER I

THE WORD "FLESH" IN THE BIBLE AND EARLY CHRISTIAN WRITINGS

Our habit of referring to the mystery of the unique and ineffable union of the Word of God with an individual human nature as the mystery of the Incarnation, and of speaking about Jesus Christ as the Word Incarnate, causes us neither difficulty nor surprise. These expressions have been among the most cherished in our Christian vocabulary for centuries, indeed, from the earliest centuries of Christianity. It may well surprise many people, then, to be told that a term of such widespread and traditional use as Incarnation really does need to be explained. We might, for example, ask ourselves whether at any time Christian people used any other terms to refer to this mystery, and if they did, how this one not merely came to be preferred to them, but eventually supplanted them altogether. It might seem at first that we have no further to go to answer this question than the brief statement of St John in the prologue to his Gospel, "And the Word was made flesh" (1. 14). But these words of St John, important as they are, do not of themselves provide us with the complete explanation for which we are looking, for to appreciate the fullness of their meaning we must see them as they would have been seen of old, on the background of a complex play and development of ideas among the Jewish people for which we shall show there is ample evidence in the Scriptures. To answer our question, then, we must begin by saying something about this development of ideas among the Jews before we say anything more about the traditional Christian use of the word *Incarnation*.[1]

THE OLD TESTAMENT

The Hebrews had a way of thinking and expressing their ideas in concrete terms: only rarely did they think abstractly or use abstract terms. This is understandable among a people who were poor, both materially and culturally, and who lived primitively first as wandering nomads, only to settle down later to the customary life of peasants. But the fact that they thought almost exclusively concretely, or in terms of the things they knew from their daily experience of life, should not lead us to imagine that they were afraid of, or incapable of serious thought. On the contrary, the Israelites, guided in their thinking by the Spirit of God, shared among themselves ideas that are so rich in meaning that they have provided the rest of mankind with many deep and enduring insights, especially into the meaning of life and death, the conditions of man's life on earth, and even into some of the most intimate of his relationships with God. An Israelite thought and expressed his ideas in terms of the events going on around him, and of what he knew of a whole series of events he conceived as making a history. The most natural medium he had for expressing his ideas was provided by the humble vocabulary he used in the course of his daily life. We could find examples to illustrate these points

[1] Some books on the Incarnation, as Karl Adam's *The Christ of Faith*, begin with a study of the Divinity of Jesus Christ. It would be indispensable for anyone interested in apologetics to begin his studies in Christology in this way. Fr Daniélou has provided such an apologetic in his recent book, *Approches du Christ*. As, however, the Divinity of Christ has already been considered in the volume of this series by Bernard Piault, *What is the Trinity?* chapters II and III, we have decided to omit matters of Trinitarian theology, and, presupposing the Divinity of the Word, to restrict our attention to the biblical uses of the word "flesh" so as to keep to the theology of the *Word Incarnate*.

from any part of the Bible, but those which come from the
beginning of the Book of Genesis are among the most striking.[2] In his account of the creation of man the sacred writer
suggests a kind of concrete definition of man as "a dust which
breathes" by bringing into his account two facts of everyday
observation, namely the return of the body to the dust of the
earth, and the holding of the breath in the nostrils. It is true
that this definition of man is not put forward in so many words
in the text of the Bible, but what we see in this definition the
Israelites of old would have seen in narrative, picturing as it
does the fingers of God modelling the clay and God's creative
breath giving life to the body his fingers were shaping as it
spread over his face. By what other means would it have been
possible to express so realistically to simple-minded people the
absolute dependence of man on God, his creator, and the
special likeness to God conferred on man by God's creative
Spirit? This striking example should help us to understand
something of the essential characteristics of a way of thinking
that was common to all the Semitic peoples of old.

Instead of using an abstract term like "human nature", or
speaking abstractly about "our human conditions of life on
earth" in writing about man, the Scriptures use what to the
Jew of old was a concrete, particular term, *flesh*. This term had
a real import about it for the ancient Semitic peoples which
our abstract terms, "man" and "human nature" cannot convey.
The word *flesh* has many different meanings in the Bible. It
denotes, sometimes in one and the same passage, (*a*) all that is
not of the bony skeleton in the human body, (*b*) a complete and
living human body, and (*c*) the earthly conditions of life which
are experienced by every frail and mortal man. The Hebrew
Basar is usually translated into Greek by σάρξ, and into Latin
by *caro*, both words being used to translate indifferently our
concrete and abstract meaning of this man, and mankind as
such. There are numerous examples we might give of these
uses of the term *flesh* in the Bible. After showing briefly that

[2] See J. L. McKenzie, *The Two-Edged Sword*, ch. i–vi.

the word came to be used by the Jews in a concrete and rich sense, we shall select a few examples of its different uses from the Old Testament. This will form the necessary introduction needed to appreciate the full meaning of the term as it is used later in the New Testament.

Firstly, the word *flesh* is frequently used in the Old Testament, in what we might call its unrestricted modern sense, to refer to the soft parts of the body covering the bones. For example, in the terrible curses uttered by God against Israel for her prevarications we read: "Will you refuse me a hearing, will you cross me, even then? If so, I will cross you in my turn, hot with anger, plaguing you sevenfold for your sins, till you must needs eat the flesh of your own sons and daughters" (Lev. 26. 27–9). The same curse is found in almost identically the same words in Deut. 28. 53. In 4 Kings the punishment inflicted on Jezabel concerns her flesh—the bones of her body will be found when the servants of Jehu go in search of the dead queen's body to bury it.

"Jezabel, he said, shall be food for dogs (dogs shall eat the flesh of Jezabel, Douay) in the purlieus of this city; in the purlieus of the city her corpse shall lie like dung on the ground, for the passers-by to wonder whether this is indeed Jezabel" (4 Kings 9. 36–7).

The prophets Jeremias (19. 9) and Baruch (2. 3) return to the curses of Leviticus and Deuteronomy speaking of "the flesh of their sons and daughters" which the prevaricating Israelites will be compelled to eat. It is, however, in the famous vision of the "dry bones" of the prophet Ezechiel that the term *flesh* is contrasted most vividly with the bony framework of the body: "A message to these bones from the Lord: I mean to send my spirit into you, and restore you to life. Sinews shall be given you, flesh shall grow on you, and skin cover you; and I will give you breath to bring you to life again; will you doubt, then, the Lord's power?" (Ezech. 37. 5–6).

This restricted sense of the word *flesh* quite naturally leads on to a more complete sense in which it is used to refer to an individual man, and also to the energy he has to expend to meet the demands that life makes on him; thus the term is used to suggest the idea of man's frailty. It is perhaps with the authors of the Sapiental Books that this fuller meaning becomes especially prominent. On many occasions the author of the Book of Job uses the word in its restricted sense, as for example in 10. 10–11: "Milk of thy milking, cheese of thy pressing, were flesh and skin that clothed me, bone and sinew that built up my frame" (see also 2. 5 and 33. 21). But in 6. 11–13 Job is surely talking about himself, and the limits of his powers of endurance, and using the word in its fuller sense: "In what strength should I hold out? In what hope repose? Have I the endurance of flint? Is my flesh brass? Help in myself is none; human aid keeps its distance from me."

The author of the Book of Proverbs also uses the word in this fuller sense in 5. 9–12 where he is advising his son to avoid all dealings with evil women: "Give not thy honour to strangers, and thy years to the cruel. Lest strangers be filled with thy strength, and thy labours be in another man's house; and thou mourn at the last, when thou shalt have spent thy flesh and thy body; and say: Why have I hated instruction, and my heart consented not to reproof . . . ?" (Douay). Similarly Ecclesiastes 12. 12: "Of making many books there is no end: and much study is an affliction of the flesh" (Douay). Of great interest is the description of a man as being "flesh and blood" (i.e. having feelings and emotions, etc., because human like the rest of men): "What of myself? Was not Solomon a mortal man like the rest of you, come down from that first man that was a thing of clay? I, too, was flesh and blood; ten months I lay a-fashioning in my mother's womb; of woman's body my stuff came, and of man's procreation; midnight joys went to the making of me" (Wisdom 7. 1–2, cf. Proverbs 12. 12). This passage is of interest because the reference it makes to the first man and his creation brings to mind the account of Genesis, the subtle influence of which can be detected in various contexts not only in different parts of the Old, but also of the New

Testament, especially the Epistles of St Paul. Looking back now once more to the account of man's creation in Genesis, we find that the word *flesh* is used in both its more restricted and its fuller sense, the former in 2. 23, and the latter in 2. 24. From the rib that God took from Adam's side, God made the woman, and on being presented with her by God Adam said: (23) "Here at last, is bone that comes from mine, flesh that comes from mine; it shall be called Woman, this thing that was taken out of man. (24) That is why man is destined to leave father and mother, and cling to his wife, instead, so that the two become *one flesh.*"

By this final expression, *one flesh*, we must certainly understand as taken for granted that, as Eve has bone and flesh which Adam recognizes as his own, man and woman are, in modern abstract terminology, one in their human nature, so that neither the distinction of their persons, nor any diversity of function or activity between them, constitutes a specific difference of nature. Human nature and human life are identical in man and woman. As man and woman are of identically the same nature, a man can take a woman to wife and the two will be united "in one flesh".

But it is perhaps in Ecclesiasticus and in the prophecies of Isaias that we come nearest to the fullness of meaning which the term *flesh* finally acquired in the New Testament, where it means the whole man in the fullness of his being and activity. Passages from Isaias using the word *flesh* were later incorporated by St Luke in his Gospel. We read in Ecclesiasticus 14. 18–19: "No living thing but fades as the grass fades (all flesh shall fade as grass, Douay); as the leaves fade, that burgeon on a growing tree, some sprouting fresh and some a-dying; so it is with flesh and blood, one generation makes room for the next." Isaias repeats the same idea in almost the same words (40. 6–8) using *flesh* to mean each and every man, as well as human life and activity: "All flesh is grass, and all the glory thereof as the flower of the field" (Douay).

Isaias prophesied that "the glory of the Lord is to be revealed for all mankind (all flesh) to see" (40. 3), and in this full sense of the term *flesh* St Luke quotes the prophecy in his Gospel (3. 6). In the Acts of the Apostles (2. 17) he quotes the prophecy of Joel (2. 32), that in the last days God would pour out his spirit "on all flesh", which Isaias had uttered earlier, saying that God would pour out his spirit on the seed and stock of his servant Jacob (44. 2–3).

By way of concluding this short survey of the Old Testament uses of the word *flesh* it is worth noting that the text of Isaias 40. 6–8 is used by the Church in the first nocturn for Matins on a Christmas Day. The liturgy never uses a passage of Scripture for a lesson on a great feast-day without intending that it should help us to meditate on the mystery of faith it is presenting to us in our prayers. The repetition of, and the contrast between the terms *word* and *flesh* in this passage of Isaias is very suggestive, indeed, too suggestive not to be intentional on the part of the inspired writer: the frailty of the flesh, of all that is human, even a complete human life, is contrasted with the eternity and the immutability of the word of God.

It would be possible to mention other passages in which the word *flesh* is used in the Old Testament, but for our purposes it is sufficient to have pointed out the uses that were traditional among the Jews, and how the word gradually came to acquire a highly complex meaning, to refer to a living man, or all living men in the completeness of their being, as well as their activities which are conditioned and limited by all manner of events that befall them. Thus the writers of the Old Testament came to endow the ancient Semitic word with the fullness of meaning with which we find it used in the New Testament.[3]

[3] M. Cazelles, quoting J. Pederson's *Israel*, I, pp. 170 ff., writes: "The Israelites were quite capable of distinguishing the soul from the body; thus for example, Isaias says: 'He shall be eaten up, body and soul' (10. 18). This may be true in a way, but the Israelites did not distinguish them as two fundamentally different manners of existing. They only distinguished the body as the weak part of man, likening it to the grass which dries up and withers, and the soul as the strong part. They

THE NEW TESTAMENT

The use that St Luke makes of the texts of Isaias and Joel we have quoted shows clearly the continuity of ideas in the use of the word *flesh* by the Old and New Testament writers. As we have said, in his Gospel (3. 6) he shows St John the Baptist making explicit references to Isaias 40: "and all mankind (all *flesh*) is to see the saving power of God." This takes us back to verse 5 of the passage from the prophet which is quoted at Christmas Matins. In the same way St Peter in his discourse at Pentecost refers to the prophecy of Joel (Acts 2. 17–21).

In his account of the prayer of Jesus after the Last Supper, St John used the word *flesh* to mean, as it means in the passages of St Luke to which we have referred, all mankind. "Glorify thy Son, that thy Son may glorify thee, as thou hast given him power over all flesh, that he may give eternal life to all whom thou hast given him" (17. 1–2, Douay). Mgr Knox translated "over all flesh" as "over all mankind".

In some passages St John uses the word *flesh* as equivalent to, or rather as involving sexual desire, as in 1. 13 and 3. 6, which we can place in parallel columns:

"Who are born, not of blood, nor of the will of the flesh, nor of the will of man, but of God" (Douay).

"That which is born of the flesh is flesh: That which is born of the Spirit is spirit" (Douay).

Very frequently, both in St John and the other writers in the New Testament, the double "flesh and blood" is used, as in the old Wisdom literature, to denote the whole man and his natural emotions and abilities. Thus our Lord assured St Peter that

regarded the soul as nobler than the body, and the body as the perfectly normal manifestation of the soul." This explains why a Hebrew could use the word *flesh* where we would use *soul*. Thus we read, for example, that it is the *flesh* which, like the heart, "rejoices in the living God" (Ps. 83. 3, Douay), which "thirsts" for God (Ps. 62. 2, Douay), which "shall have pain" (Job 14. 22, Douay), or, on the contrary, "shall rest in hope" (Ps. 15. 9, Douay). The *flesh* receives and loses life (Prov. 14. 30), and it is involved in sin (Eccles. 5. 5). Finally, in one text from Leviticus (13. 18) *the flesh* probably means an individual man.

"it is not flesh and blood, it is my Father in heaven that has revealed this to thee" (Matt. 16. 17). Similarly, St Paul wrote to the Galatians that when God had called him "to reveal his Son in me, that I might preach him among the Gentiles; immediately I condescended not to flesh and blood" (1. 16, Douay), which Mgr Knox translated as concluding "my first thought was not to hold any consultation with any human creature". Again, writing to the Ephesians, St Paul says that: "It is not against (creatures of) flesh and blood that we enter the lists; we have to do with princedoms and powers, with those who have the mastery of the world in these dark days, with malign influences in an order higher than our own" (6. 12).

We have emphasized the realism and fullness of meaning with which the word *flesh* is used concretely in these and other passages first of the Old, and then of the New Testaments, so that, with this preliminary work in mind, we might turn to consider the reality of the *flesh* which the Word of God took to himself. It would not be difficult to select texts from the New Testament in which the reality of the body and the complete human nature of Christ is definitely set before us by the use of this word which the sacred writers took over from the vocabulary of the Old Testament and used like a technical term. We can give here in an approximate chronological order a few of the most striking of these texts.

The earliest New Testament writings emphasize unfailingly the reality of Christ's body when they are speaking about the central event of his whole life, his passion and death. Thus, St Peter, in his discourse on the day of Pentecost, while insisting on God's foreknowledge, cites Psalm 15. 9, "moreover my flesh also shall rest in hope", and declares that David "was a prophet, and he knew God had promised him on oath that he would set the sons of his body upon the throne; it was of the Christ he said, foreseeing his resurrection, that he was not left in the place of death, and that his body (flesh) did not see corruption" (Acts 2. 30–1).

In his Epistles St Peter insists on the human and temporal reality of our Lord, for his suffering as a man is basic to the mystery of salvation. He writes, "Christ's mortal nature (flesh), then, has been crucified, and you must arm yourselves with the same intention; he whose mortal nature (flesh) has been crucified is quit, now, of sin. The rest of your mortal life (life in the flesh) must be ordered by God's will, not by human appetites" (1 Peter 4. 1–2).

The use of the expression "in the flesh" here is particularly worthy of note, for besides meaning "mortal nature", or living body in which Christ wrought our redemption on the cross (verse 1), it is also used to mean our human way of living on earth (verse 1), as in many of the Old Testament texts. Thus "Christ's mortal nature" in verse 1 means his full human nature, not merely his body. St Paul writes in the same kind of way especially about the body of Christ as the instrument of our salvation. Three important texts will suffice to show this:

> He is our bond of peace; he has made the two nations one, breaking down the wall that was a barrier between us, the enmity there was between us, in his own mortal nature [in his flesh] (Ephes. 2. 14).
>
> You, too, were once estranged from him; your minds were alienated from him by a life of sin; but now he has used Christ's natural body to win you back through his death [he hath reconciled you in the body of his flesh through death—Douay] (Col. 1. 21–2).
>
> We are limbs of his body; flesh and bone, we belong to him [or in the Douay version:] For we are members of his body, of his flesh and of his bones (Ephes. 5. 30).

But it is St John who, last of all in time, and with a vigour intensified by his reaction to the Docetist heresy,[4] emphasized in the most forthright manner he could that his uses of the term

---

[4] See Karl Adam, *The Christ of Faith*, pp. 28–30. "According to the view of the Docetae, Jesus' entire human nature is mere outward appearance: his body is appearance, his suffering is appearance" (p. 28).

flesh, so far from being a concession to an imperfection of language, was perfectly deliberate for, as used in his day, it was the precise word required to express the unquestionable reality of Christ's manhood.

Every Christian knows how St John used the word *flesh* in the remarkable formula of the mystery of the Incarnation in the prologue to his Gospel: "The Word was made flesh, and came to dwell among us" (1. 14). With these words St John puts before his readers the Word of God in the completeness of the human nature he took to himself, with its human ways of acting as well as its human limitations and frailties. This is, indeed, a sentence which "means more for mankind than any sentence ever written by a human pen".[5] As we read this text of St John we recall quite naturally the Old Testament notion of "the flesh" it portrayed man as being. St John is using the Old Testament word for "man" to write about Christ. As we read John 1. 14 familiar passages from the Old Testament echo in our minds: "And God said: My spirit shall not remain in man for ever, because he is flesh" (Genesis 6. 3, Douay), and, "In God I will praise my words, in God I have put my trust, I will not fear what flesh can do against me" (Psalm 55. 5, Douay). As we read St John's prologue we ought also to remember that this important formula, "The Word was made flesh", stating in so few words the mystery of the Incarnation, is the focal point on which several currents of Jewish thought from the Old Testament, such as those associated with the Logos-Wisdom, with the divine Presence within the Tabernacle, and with the spirituality of the *Shekinah*, converge to meet with others coming from the New Testament revelation of Christ and the Blessed Trinity. The alliteration between the Hebrew word *shekinah* and the Greek word ἐσκήνωσεν (he dwelt or "tented" amongst us) has not escaped the notice of scholars. The Temple, which is the embodiment of the divine

[5] W. Leonard, "St John's Gospel" in *A Catholic Commentary on Holy Scripture*, col. 783c.

schékinâh, is, for St John, the flesh of the son of man (cf. 2. 21).[6]

St John returns once again, at the beginning of his first Epistle, to emphasize the reality of the "Word of life which was in the beginning" coming in the flesh, and he does so with such insistence that there can be no doubt he had in mind the heresy of the Docetae, for whom the Incarnation was not a reality but a mere appearance and pretence.[7] This seems to be the only way of accounting for the extraordinary repetition of words connected with human sense experiences:

> Our message concerns the Word, who is life;
> what he was from the first, what we have heard about him,
> what our own eyes have seen of him;
> what it was that met our gaze, and the touch of our hands.
> Yes, life dawned, and it is as eye-witnesses that we give you news of that life, that eternal life, which ever abode with the Father and has dawned, now, on us.
>
> (1 John 1. 1–2)

Again in the same Epistle (4. 1–2): "Many false prophets have made their appearance in the world. This is the test by which God's Spirit is to be recognized; every spirit which acknowledges Jesus Christ as having come to us in human flesh has God for its author."

ST PAUL

The use of the word *flesh* in the vocabulary of St Paul calls for special consideration on its own.

The theory is sometimes advanced that Paul's doctrine about man, and especially his use of the pair, "the flesh and the

---

[6] See Bouyer, *Bible et Vie Chrétienne*, 20, "The Schékinâh: God with us." This is echoed by St Paul when he writes, for example, that "in Christ the whole plenitude of Deity is embodied, and dwells in him" (Col. 2. 9). See *A Catholic Commentary on Holy Scripture*, col. 783b.

[7] "Many false teachers have appeared in the world, who will not acknowledge that Jesus Christ has come in human flesh" (2 John 7).

spirit", was borrowed from Greek philosophy, though not all who propose this theory are agreed whether he was well or ill advised in borrowing his ideas from such a source. Fr Prat considers that, whatever he owed to Greek philosophy, this theory cannot apply to St Paul's doctrine about man which is inspired solely by the Bible.[8] For one thing Paul has the unphilosophical, but characteristically biblical way of gliding imperceptibly from one shade of meaning to another when he uses the word *flesh*; sometimes he uses it to mean a living organism (so that he always has the soul in mind when he writes about the *flesh*),[9] and at other times he uses it to mean a man's way of living on earth, or the physical and moral frailty of man's nature. It is, in fact, impossible to decide on the exact sense in which he is using the term in a passage which is taken out of its context, such is the freedom he allows himself in the uses he finds for it. Thus it would be a serious error to attribute to him a kind of cryptic or unconscious Manicheism on the strength of isolated texts in which he opposes the weakness of the flesh to the sanctity of the spirit.

But—and this is the point of special interest to us—"it is certain that St Paul gives to Christ a flesh similar to our own, and that he nevertheless denies that Christ has anything to do with sin. This proves clearly that sin is not inherent in the flesh from which it is inseparable."[10] Thus in the passage in 2 Cor. (5. 21) we read that: "Christ never knew sin, and God made him into sin for us, so that in him we might be turned into the holiness of God" [i.e. Christ was made the scapegoat for our sins], and in Hebrews 4. 15: "It is not as if our high priest was incapable of feeling for us in our humiliations; he has been through every trial, fashioned as we are, only sinless." Though he does not use the word *flesh* in either passage, nonetheless, basing himself on the principle expressed later, *quod non est assumptum, non est sanatum*, St Paul gives the equality of

[8] See F. Prat, S.J., *The Theology of Saint Paul*, II, pp. 69–76.
[9] See F. Prat, *op. cit.*, p. 71.
[10] See F. Prat, *op. cit.*, p. 70.

Christ's human nature with our own as the reason why the Father made him, the Just One, undergo in the flesh,[11] and in our place, the penalty merited by us sinners in our own flesh. In Romans 8. 3 he states this famous principle of the theology of the Redemption: "There was something the law could not do, because flesh and blood could not lend it the power; and this God has done, by sending his own Son, in the fashion of our guilty nature, to make amends for our guilt."

The reality of Christ's human nature is also put forward by St Paul in the way he likens Christ's birth to that of man, and indeed of a Jew (cf. Gal. 3. 15–16). He writes of God's Son "descended, in respect of his human birth, from the line of David" (Rom. 1. 3), and he tells the Galatians that "God sent out his Son on a mission to us. He took birth from a woman, took birth as a subject of the law" (Gal. 4. 4).

St Paul insists so forcefully on the genuine reality of Christ's body and entire human nature that at the beginning of the Epistle to the Colossians he invents a curious pleonasm while he is explaining how it is that Christ is above all created beings: "And you, whereas you were some time alienated and enemies in mind in evil works: Yet now he hath reconciled *in the body of his flesh* through death, to present you holy and unspotted and blameless before him" (1. 21–2, Douay). The expression *the body of his flesh* translates the Greek ἐν τῷ σώματι τῆς σαρκός. St Paul presents the same ideas of Christ reconciling all men to the Father in the sufferings he bore in the *flesh* in the Epistle to the Ephesians, but contents himself with the use of the word σάρξ, *flesh* (2. 14–16).

The reader can see for himself easily enough that in the passages we have quoted the bad sense of the word *flesh*, found frequently in the Stoic schools of philosophy, does not dominate, nor permeate every use of the word as it is used by St Paul.[12] In his mind the word *flesh* denotes in most contexts, as

[11] See below, ch. v, pp. 120 following.
[12] See F. Prat, *op. cit.*, pp. 401–7. "Certain phrases of the Old Testament tended to give the word *flesh* a derogatory meaning: Genesis 6. 3 and 12. The philosophical language of the Stoics had a similar tendency.

we have pointed out it does generally in the Bible, living matter, a living human body (especially in texts referring to circumcision), and thence human nature with man's experience of his frailty; he uses it also in stating facts about human descent and natural kinship, all of which are inseparably associated with the life of an individual man, and finally to denote human nature as we know it to be in the existing order of things, tainted by sin and infected by concupiscence.[13] But the texts we have cited show decisively that St Paul never had this final meaning in mind when he used the word *flesh* with reference to Jesus Christ. On the contrary, he explicitly set it aside (see 2 Cor. 5. 21). The reality of Christ's earthly or incarnate being is necessarily conjoined with the sanctity of his flesh or human nature, and it is this sanctity which saves us and our sinful bodily natures from sin and death. The connection between sin and the flesh is thus not essential. Manichean and Docetist ideas about the human body are incompatible with the doctrine of the Incarnation of the Word of God, the eternal Son of the Father "who was made to him of the seed of David, according to the flesh" (Rom. 1. 3).

THE WRITINGS OF THE EARLY CHRISTIANS

The scriptural term *flesh*, which occurs so prominently in the New Testament, is, as one might quite naturally expect, used in the writings of the early Christians in the same kind of way as it was used in the Bible. The earliest Christian writers love to show how, by the abasement and humility of his life on earth, the Word made his love for mankind clearly known. The few examples that we give here from some early Christian writers have been selected from the article entitled "Incarnation" by Mgr A. Michel in the *Dictionnaire de Théologie*

After Epicurus had made the flesh the seat of pleasure and pain and the source of bliss, the Stoics did their best to depreciate the flesh. The proof of this is found in Seneca, Plutarch, Marcus Aurelius and especially in Epictetus, who takes pleasure in designating the flesh by a contemptuous diminutive σαρκίδιον" (p. 402).

[13] See F. Prat, *op. cit.*, pp. 402–3.

Catholique[14] and the selection has been made merely to show the equivalence flesh=body, and flesh=individual man, which they adopted following the biblical vocabulary.

The Epistle of Barnabas states that Jesus delivered "his flesh", that is to say, his body (v, 1; vi, 3; vii, 5), and that he appeared "in the flesh" (v, 6; vii, 7; xii, 10), and that he came "in the flesh" (v, 10; 11). Pope St Clement in his *Epistle to the Corinthians* (xxxii, 2) uses the expression ὁ κύριος ᾽Ιησοῦς τὸ κατὰ σάρκα to refer to Christ considered as man, and also the same expression is used by St Ignatius of Antioch in his *Epistle to the Magnesians* (xiii, 2). Continuing the struggle against Docetism commenced by St John and these first writers, especially as it appeared with the Gnostics, St Irenaeus identified the terms *flesh* and *man* in the earliest effort to express the mystery of the Incarnation in a clear formula. In his *Against the Heresies* (Book 3, ch. xviii, no. 7) he stated that the formula "The Word was made flesh" means that "The Word was made man". He argues that if the Word had not been made flesh, he would only have had the appearance of being in the flesh, and then the work of God would not have been genuine. The man which he appeared to be, Jesus was in reality. In him and by him God recapitulated, or restored the very nature of man he had given originally to Adam. In chapter xix he coins our technical word *Incarnation*, σάρκωσις, this being the first time that the term was used. After the time of St Irenaeus the word and its normal Greek derivatives σαρκωθέν, he who is incarnated, σαρκωθείς, being incarnate, become more and more generally used by Greek writers. Aristides says that the Word of God, took flesh, σάρκα ἀνέλαβεν of the Virgin (*Apologia*, 15). In the West, Tertullian, identifying the words *flesh* and *man*, speaks of the Word Incarnate (*De Carne Christi*, 5; *Adversus Praxeas*, ch. 27). If St Clement of Alexandria was content to say that the Word took flesh, or was clothed with flesh (*Stromata*, vi, ch. 15), Origen states explicitly *homo factus incarnatus est*:

[14] See col. 1446–53.

being made man he was incarnated (*De Principiis*, 1, praef. no. 4).

Thus by the end of the third century the word *Incarnation* was being widely used and was well on the way to being accepted universally by Christians.

During the controversies occasioned by Apollinarianism, however, the traditional use of the word *flesh* brought the completeness of Christ's human nature into question for the first time. Apollinaris of Laodicea (died about A.D. 390), held that the Word assumed not a complete human nature formed of body and soul, but only a body informed by a lower, sensuous soul without any higher, spiritual or intellectual soul. He considered the activities an ordinary man owes to his mind and will were performed by Christ, not by a human mind and will, but by the Divine Word himself supplying for the higher spiritual soul.[15] The opposite view was taken a little later by the Nestorians who, arguing that the term *flesh* must be taken to refer to a complete man, refused to say that the human nature of Jesus is the "human nature of God"; they maintained that in Christ the man is a complete unity or whole, an entire body-soul unit distinct from, but conjoined in a close moral union to the divine Nature of the Word.[16] In other words, the Son of God was closely united to, and did not literally become a man. The Word merely dwelt in the man as in a temple. The Fathers reacted against these heretical ideas by insisting on the equivalence of the term σάρκωσις or *incarnation*, and ἐνανθρωπήσις, which can only be translated as *being made man* (hominization). They took their stand on the teaching of the Council of Nicea, which had already defined against the Arians the bodily reality of the Word Incarnate, who in being flesh was made a complete man. The different formulas coined by the Fathers could be set out line by line, as they are in the article of Mgr Michel, but it would be tiresome for us to reproduce them here. The one point that we must grasp firmly,

---

[15] See ch. 11. Also Karl Adam, *op. cit.*, pp. 30–4.
[16] See ch. 11. Also, Karl Adam, *op. cit.*, pp. 35–8.

because it stands out in the writings of all the Fathers of this period, is the constancy with which the Church stood by the formula of St John, "The Word was made flesh", and the persistence with which she used the recently coined term, *Incarnation*; this formula of St John, and this term derived from it, were reminders to all the faithful, firstly of the love of God for man which Christ showed in the flesh, and secondly of God's motive for becoming a man, namely to redeem us all from sin, our flesh or human nature being the source of our sinful condition. St Augustine later summarized the ideas which the Fathers of this period wished to preserve by the use of this special word in one of those magnificent epigrams which flowed so effortlessly and so frequently from his pen: "The flesh has blinded you; but the flesh cures you, because Christ has come in the flesh to extinguish the passion of the flesh."[17]

The dogmatic formulas of the Church finally ratified the treatment of the expressions *caro factus* and *homo factus*, made flesh and *made man*, as equivalent. The Apostles' Creed had only declared that Jesus was born of the Virgin Mary. The Creed of Nicea (A.D. 325) and Constantinople (A.D. 381), however, used both terms to refer to the union of the divine and human natures of the Son of Mary.[18] Thus the Greeks had at their disposal two terms by which to refer to the mystery while the less subtle but scientifically more secure Latin compelled the Western Church to keep to the one term *Incarnation*, or made flesh.

There are, then, two different senses in which we can speak of the mystery of the Incarnation: (*a*) *in an active sense*: with reference to the act by which God took to himself human nature in the womb of the Virgin Mary, to make it subsist in the Second Person of the Blessed Trinity, the Word; (*b*) *in a passive sense*: with reference to the unique and wondrous union of the divine and human natures in the one Person of the Word. Without ceasing to be the Word, the divine Person

---

[17] St Augustine, *Homilies on St John's Gospel*, 2, 16.
[18] See Denzinger-Bannwart, 54 and 86.

of the Son possesses as his own a perfect human nature, so that he is God and man.

If Scripture, as God's own declaration about himself, cannot be challenged, it is quite clear that the persistent use of the word *flesh* in connection with the coming of the Word of God, and its interpretation by the Fathers and by the Church herself in her teaching about the Incarnation, ought to remove any trace of doubt or misunderstanding about the reality of the true manhood of Jesus Christ. The word *Incarnation* suggests the whole biblical message about the Person of Christ.

But if he has a need to receive and be taught what he is to believe for salvation, man has also an irrepressible need to understand; even if he cannot approach close to the burning bush in which the mystery of God appears to us, he must at least think the mystery as correctly as he is humanly able, especially if he is going to identify himself with it as far as he can so as to associate himself with the work of the Church in making the mystery of Christ known to others.[19]

[19] Before passing on to chapter II, the reader who is fortunate enough to possess a copy of volume II of Newman's *Parochial and Plain Sermons* would be well advised to study carefully Sermon 3 which is on the Incarnation.

THE MYSTERY OF THE HYPOSTATIC UNION: THE CRUCIAL PROBLEMS OF CHRISTOLOGY

Before we enter into the intricacies of the theological exposition of the mystery of the Word Incarnate, we need to have some understanding of the great issues that were at stake in the controversies and complex struggles concerning the doctrine of the hypostatic union and the Person of Jesus Christ which went on with little respite from the first half of the fifth till the middle of the seventh century. A knowledge of the actual historical sequence of events, which played a part in shaping the Catholic doctrine of the hypostatic union of the divine and human natures in Christ, will help the reader to realize that the central problems involved in any effort to think about Jesus Christ are to be met by keeping to a path which lies roughly midway between the two extreme errors of Nestorianism, condemned at the Council of Ephesus in 431 on the one hand, and Eutychianism or Monophysitism, condemned at the Council of Chaledon in 451, on the other. Thus no one should feel surprised if in this chapter we restrict our attention to the history of these two great heresies which arose and raged like conflagrations in the middle of the fifth century. By way of introduction, however, it will be useful to take a brief glance at certain errors which appeared previously, and in a way prepared for the supreme crises of the fifth century. Finally, before concluding this chapter, it will be as well to say something in a very general way about the manner in which, since the time of Laelius Socinius († 1562), and his nephew Faustus Socinius († 1604), who attacked the mysteries of faith in the name of reason, and more especially since the development of the thoroughgoing rationalism of the nineteenth century, Jesus Christ has been regarded by many people in modern times.

ERRORS PRECEDING THE GREAT CHRISTOLOGICAL CRISES OF THE FIFTH CENTURY

Docetism

From the earliest times the idea of the incarnation of a god has haunted the minds of men but, as it has baffled their imagination and understanding, they have never succeeded in thinking seriously nor consistently about it. We need not, then, be altogether surprised that the very first generations of Christian people saw a movement develop which denied the truth of the Incarnation of the Word by denying the reality of the body of Christ. This movement became known as Docetism because it taught that Christ's body was only apparently real. Its adherents were firmly convinced that Christ was God, but they were scandalized at the thought of God living and suffering as a mere man, especially in the way that Christ lived and suffered. They sought the solution of their difficulties simply but naïvely, by saying that the Word only appeared as a man and only seemed to have a body. During the second century Docetism was spread by the Gnostics who regarded matter as evil and the fabrication of some demiurge; they held as a consequence that God could not take flesh to himself.[1] We have already noted how St John fought the errors of the Docetae, and the reaction of the Apostolic Fathers to their theories was

[1] See L. Cristiani, *Heresies and Heretics*, in this series, pp. 12–15, which is very relevant to this chapter.

no less marked than that of the Beloved Disciple. St Ignatius of Antioch, for example, wrote to the Trallians emphasizing the genuine reality of Christ's human nature:

> Stop your ears when one speaks to you apart from Jesus Christ, who is of the race of David, the child of Mary, who was truly born and ate and drank, was truly persecuted by Pontius Pilate, was truly crucified and died, before the eyes of those in heaven and those on earth and those under the earth; Who also was truly raised from the dead.[2]

In most of his Epistles St Ignatius returns time and again to rebut the errors of Docetism, for they struck at the very heart of Catholic doctrine. How, he asked, could it be said that mankind has been ransomed, if the sufferings of our Saviour were not true sufferings, and if he had never been a real man? How could we speak of a Saviour at all if Christ had never lived or died as a man?

The theorizings of the Docetae did not lack a certain plausibility for some minds, and the technique they employed in expounding their theories was so popular that they scarcely ever varied it. Men of all ages are familiar with the theme, beloved by certain eager hunters after a special kind of mystery story, of the substitution of someone else for the condemned person at the moment of the infliction of punishment. The Docetae propagated the story that Simon of Cyrene was the man who was really crucified in the place of Jesus who, having slipped from the crowd unseen, disappeared by ascending into heaven. In modern times, some writers have held in the same way that at the last moment someone else was slipped into Joan of Arc's place and died in her stead on the pyre in Rouen. Other Docetae, mixing philosophy with history, held that the "pneumatic" or "spiritual" Christ was separated from the "psychic" or "human" Christ, not before death, but from the commencement of the Passion, in such a way that the true Christ, the Word of God, never died at all.

[2] St Ignatius, *Epistle to the Trallians*, ix (trans. by J. A. Kleist).

Because of its excessive simplicity Docetism has often been a temptation even for orthodox Christians. During the first centuries of Christianity certain expressions, more or less suspect of tending towards Docetism in one way or another, appeared in the works of several writers. Thus, for example, Clement of Alexandria wrote that it would be ridiculous to believe that the Saviour had any need to care for, or even to nourish, his body in order to conserve its existence. If Jesus ate, this was not on account of any need of his own, but out of consideration for those with whom he lived, lest they might come to think, as some people did later on, that he had nothing more than the appearance of a body.[3] Clement rejected Docetism as a theory, but his way of thinking about Christ's human nature, and his way of expressing his ideas were confused; his statements about Christ as a man reveal a kind of cryptic or unconscious Docetism on his part. Such a statement as "because of the weak, I became weak; because of those who hunger, I hungered; because of those who thirst, I thirsted",[4] was not strictly speaking Docetist in intention, but if isolated from its context, and presented without further explanation, it is certainly ambiguous in meaning, and could easily be construed as Docetist by implication. These examples show that it is possible to glorify Christ as God in such a way as to fall all too easily into the snare of playing down the reality of his human nature, and by treating it as above human necessities to veer towards a disguised form of Docetism.

Arianism

Other heretics tried to rob Christ altogether, not of his human nature, but of his divinity. The first of these great heresies in time—formidable in quite different ways and for very different reasons to Docetism—aimed at nothing less than denying that Christ was really the Word of God. Arius held that all that is said to be God or of God in Jesus is in fact inferior to the

[3] St Clement of Alexandria, *Stromata*, VI, ch. 9, no. 71.
[4] Origen, *Commentary on St Matthew's Gospel*, 13, a.

eternal and unbegotten God. Christ is only divine in a secondary kind of way. In other words, he is not literally divine at all. The person of the Word which St John had placed in him was never, according to Arius, consubstantial with the Father. The heresy of Arius attacks, then, directly and immediately the doctrine of the Trinity, for it denies that the Father has a Son who is his Word consubstantial with himself.

Arius reproduced the teaching of Lucian of Antioch:

> Lucian had insisted above all on the unity of the eternal, unbegotten God. He declared, by contrast, that the Word had been formed from nothing, that there had been a time when he had not existed, that he had been engendered not necessarily, but freely by the Father. He could safely conclude from this that the Word, though not eternal, was not a creature in the same way as other beings; he could even bring clearly into relief his rôle in the creation of the world, and declare that he was even an image of the οὐσία (essence), will, power and glory of the Father. It would be difficult for Arius to avoid the conclusion that the Father alone deserved to be called God in the strict sense of the word, and that the Word was only, by comparison, a subordinate and accessory divinity. In the Trinity as Arius conceived it there might be three persons, but they could only be one by the harmony of their wills, and not one in nature.[5]

Thus, on this theory, the Word who became man is, in any case, not God.

Arianism bore witness to the continuing survival of Gnosticism in that it presented the man Jesus as being at the top of a long line of created beings called Aeons, the first and highest of which were the Logos and the Holy Spirit. This conception of a complex hierarchy of created things originated from the Greek practice of treating a chain of closely linked concepts or ideas as equivalent to a series of different realities linked together like the ideas. The Gnostics seem to have indulged in this way of thinking, and associated with their ideas of creation

[5] G. Bardy, *Histoire de l'Eglise*, edited by Fliche and Martin, III, p. 72.

a good deal of pagan mythology and polytheism. There is no doubt that polytheism, and philosophical ideas derived from remote Platonic sources, were rife in Asian, and especially Gnostic circles at the time.

After its condemnation at the Council of Nicea (in 325) Arianism continued to survive under fresh disguises, one of which found expression in the errors of Apollinaris of Laodicea, a theologian of the school of Alexandria, and another in the theories of Nestorius, both of whom were in fact professedly strongly anti-Arian. According to Apollinaris the Word, who is consubstantial with the Father, took, as St Paul said, "the form of a servant". But God could not take a body informed by a soul because a soul-body unity is a complete individual human person, and a human person cannot be God himself. Thus Christ could not have two complete natures, for if he had two natures, the Word as one Person would only have been within a man as the other. In order, then, to have, in the unity of his one being and nature, the reality of Christ's physical body and the reality of the Word with his divine nature, Apollinaris considered that the Word, the Logos, took a human body without any spiritual soul, and that in Christ the Word himself supplied for the spiritual soul. Apollinaris expressed his idea of the nature of the Word Incarnate in a formula that was shortly to become the centre of bitter quarrels: he said that Christ is "the one nature of the God-Logos become flesh". Arius had advocated this theory in the first place in order to be able to attribute to the Word, the Person of Jesus, the imperfections in knowledge and the hesitations of will which the Gospel reveals in Christ, and thence deny that Jesus is God. For example, Christ declared that he, the Word of God, did not know the time of the last judgement (Mark 13. 32); during the Agony in the Garden he was troubled in spirit "and sorrowful even unto death", and he admitted that not he, but the Father alone is good (Matt. 19. 17): Arius concluded that passages from the Gospels like these showed plainly that Christ, the Word, is inferior to the unbegotten

Father who alone is God. The Fathers who wrote against Arius, and Apollinaris himself, did not fail to note that Christ, in speaking in this way, and in suffering as he did, was speaking and suffering "as man", and not "as God", but at this period they experienced considerable difficulty in explaining the meaning of this distinction.

St Athanasius, the patriarch of Alexandria, on returning from exile in 362, tried to arrest the spread of Apollinarianism. A profession of faith was drawn up to serve as a basis to bring about a reconciliation between the Apollinarists and their adversaries, the most formidable of whom came from the rival theology school of Antioch. The Apollinarists stood firmly by their view that it is impossible to liken the presence of the Word in Christ to that of God in his prophets, for this would destroy the unity of Christ's being, while the Antiochean theologians insisted that, as he redeemed both the body and the soul of man, Christ must have had both a human body and a human soul, and so have been a complete and perfect man. The Logos, while remaining true God, had become also a real man. A profession of faith in Christ as God and man would, it was hoped, bring the controversy which had begun to an end: no one, alas, realized that the disagreements were only just beginning. The incredible resourcefulness and subtlety of the Eastern mind had not yet found full scope to display its capabilities, but, as the scene changed from Alexandria to Constantinople, it was to be provided with abundant scope.

THE HERESY OF NESTORIUS AND THE COUNCIL OF EPHESUS (431)

Introduction

After the death of the second successor of St John Chrysostom, one of the greatest of the patriarchs of Constantinople, the personal ambitions of a number of rival candidates for the see threatened to create such a state of confusion, that the emperor, Theodosius II, resorted to the standard process to meet the emergency by stepping in and offering the see to a man he trusted, who, as it happened, was unknown to the local clergy. In a monastery near Antioch there was a priest of considerable renown for virtue and eloquence who ruled his monks with prudence and skill. His name was Nestorius. Called from Antioch to occupy the See of Constantinople, just as St John Chrysostom had been thirty years before in circumstances remarkably similar, the new patriarch was consecrated bishop at the beginning of April, 428.[6]

As soon as he embarked upon his duties he wrote a letter to the pope, St Celestine, to express his desire to be at one with the pope, and to safeguard the unity of the true faith threatened as it was by many heresies. The Creed of Nicea had checked the progress of a dangerous rationalism that had threatened to inundate the Christian world. Arius had aimed at nothing less than reducing the Word of God to the status of a creature, superior to all other creatures, out of a substance inferior to God. Everything which in any way savoured of Arianism was, after the Council of Nicea, rightfully suspect by orthodox Catholics. Nestorius, however, accepting wholeheartedly the doctrine of the Trinity and the divinity of the Word of God, was worried about the ways in which people were coming to speak about the temporal and earthly birth of Christ. The Word of God, whom the Council of Nicea had acknowledged as consubstantial with, and born eternally from the Father, was now being said to have been born of the Virgin Mary: she was as a consequence being hailed with the title *Theotokos*, Mother of God. This title was admittedly not new, but it was not to be found in the Scriptures, and it had not been acknowledged by the Fathers at Nicea. In speaking of the Virgin Mary in this way, Nestorius argued, it was impossible to avoid confusing, when thinking about the Word Incarnate, the divine and human natures of the Son of God. Many were evidently forgetting that the Council of Nicea had defined that the Lord Jesus Christ, Son of God, was born of the Holy Spirit and of the Virgin

[6] See Philip Hughes, *History of the Church*, I, ch. 9.

Mary, so that he had two natures: that of the Son of God consubstantial with the Father, and that of man, born of Mary,
which we should adore together.

Plainly enough, such a way of speaking could, despite its
vagueness and imprecision, be given a rigorously orthodox
interpretation. The difficulties to which it gave rise, and of
which Nestorius was well aware, lie in the way in which it
presents the union of the two natures which, he said, exist, and
are to be adored together because both are complete. As the
two natures are complete, and as they exist *together*, Nestorius
came to the conclusion that in Christ there are two persons,
the divine Person of the Word, and the person of the man Jesus,
united together in a harmony of will, so that the Person of the
Word merely dwells within the human person of Jesus as in a
temple.

The difficulties experienced by the patriarch seem to have
been fatally aggravated by the confusion in terminology which
was becoming universal at the time among the theologians of
the Greek-speaking world. The root of the trouble lay in the
fact that the theologians of the two rival schools of theology,
the one at Antioch and the other at Alexandria, had no clear
understanding of each other's terms, and they differed in their
ways of considering the two natures of Christ, the Word Incarnate. The growing confusion about the very meaning of the
term "nature" was bearing fruit in the different interpretations
that were being put on Mary's title of Mother of God or
Theotokos and this reflected the conflicting ideas about the
union of natures in Christ.

Both Nestorius and his adversaries had in mind the necessity
both of professing the divinity and consubstantiality of the
Word of God with God the Father, and of accepting the condemnation incurred by Apollinaris of Laodicea by St Damascus
in 375 and at the first Council of Constantinople in 381. As
we have said Apollinaris had used a formula in speaking of the
unity of Christ's being which was regarded as highly question-
able: "the one nature of the God-Logos become flesh". The

Church had condemned his theory attempting to account for the union of the human and divine natures in Christ, and had insisted that Christ has two natures, but in her documents she neither condemned his formula nor had she given any account of how these two natures are united in Christ. The documents of the Church simply stated the reality of their union, and cautioned theologians about the necessity of avoiding the opposite excess to that of Apollinaris, that is, of speaking of two Christs, one of whom would be the Son of God and the other the son of man: *there is only one Christ and one Son, but this one Christ has two natures*. And now in 428 Nestorius was proclaiming the divinity of the Word, and rejecting Apollinarianism by advocating the distinction of two natures in Christ; but he was pressing this distinction so far as to say that Mary was not the Mother of God, of the Person of the Word in Jesus Christ; she was only the Mother of the man Jesus. Was this, or was it not, tantamount to saying that there are really two persons in Christ?

We must say a word now about the theological outlook of the rival schools of Alexandria and Antioch, which at this time regarded each other with deep suspicion and distrust not merely for theological, but also for calamitous political reasons.

The school of Alexandria remained faithful to the teaching of the great St Athanasius. His Christology could be summarized in a formula more mystical than scientific in character: "God was made man in order that man might thereby become divine." To safeguard the consubstantiality of the Word with the Father, defended with such vehemence by the most illustrious of all its patriarchs, the masters of this school tended to shade down the active rôle of Christ's human nature and merge it within that of the divine nature. In their view of the Incarnation the human nature of the Incarnate Word did not disappear, so they could not be accused of Docetism or of denying that Christ had two natures; the Apollinarian distinctions between a man with only a sensuous soul and a man with an intellectual soul were abandoned, so they professed to hold that Christ's human nature was complete and unimpaired in its integrity. But they held that the rôle of the human nature counted for the least in Christ's activities: the activity of the Word was treated by them as of paramount and well-nigh exclusive importance. For example St Athanasius, in his treatise on the "Incarnation of the Word of God", is particularly anxious to show the pre-eminence of the rôle of the Word. The following extract from the second chapter provides us with an excellent illustration of his way of thinking:

> He, the Mighty One, the Artificer of all, himself prepared this body in the Virgin as a temple for himself, and took it for his very own, as the instrument through which he was known and in which he dwelt. Thus, taking a body like our own, because all our bodies were liable to the corruption of death, he surrendered his body to death instead of all, and offered it to the Father.... This he did that he might turn again to incorruption men who had turned back to corruption, and make them alive through death by the appropriation of his body and by the grace of his resurrection. Thus he would make death to disappear from them as utterly as straw from fire.[7]

For St Athanasius it is the Logos, the Word of God, who is at once the Saviour from sin, the Master of man's mind, and the deifier of human nature which he reinstated before God the Father. St Athanasius' mind moved, it may be observed, on the level of metaphysical ideas, and descended from this height to view the world of facts. He and his successors had one and the same supreme objective and it was to put into clear relief the absolute supremacy of the Word over all those whom he had come to rescue from sin, error and death. The school of Alexandria was always intent on showing forth the reality of God, and the divinity of the Word in Christ, especially in all his activities; for this school he seemed to act more as God than as man.[8]

[7] St Athanasius, *De Incarnatione Verbi*, Book 2, sect. 2 (trans. by a Religious of C.S.M.V., p. 34).
[8] See Hughes, *op. cit.*, p. 237. Karl Adam, *op. cit.*, p. 34.

At Antioch, on the other hand, the masters and their numerous disciples were more interested in exegesis than in speculative theology and metaphysics; they prized before everything else the closest possible adherence to, and the literal explanation of the text of the Gospels. Arius had made a point of emphasizing and building all his theology on the contradictory statements which are to be found in various texts of the Gospels about the Person of Christ. This method of exegesis was fraught with dangers of which by this time everyone was well aware. The theologians at Antioch, therefore, in their presentation of the mystery of the Word Incarnate, distinguished carefully the texts which refer to the man Jesus Christ from those which refer to the divine Word who became man. They held that

> the Word, in Jesus Christ, was united to a man, but he neither modified nor changed this man. The Word came to him, and dwelt with him: the Word was not mixed nor blended with the man. The union of the Word with the human nature can, then, be explained in two ways: either the Word came to Jesus in a manner similar to that in which the Holy Spirit came down on the prophets, so that he was united to the man by love and good will, or the Word resided in Jesus in such a way that after the union there is only one, and no more than one centre of activity and attribution, one single person.[9]

The second of these alternatives could be taken as the basis for an orthodox interpretation of the mystery of the Incarnate Word more readily than the first, and it is in fact akin to the conception of the union of the divine and human natures held by the theologians of Alexandria. But the theologians at Antioch found difficulties with this view as soon as they tried to show *how* the union was established. Nestorius, in particular, from the start adopted the first of the alternatives, for it was more in keeping with the teaching of the Antiochean doctors who were "concerned to safeguard the all important truth of the real distinction between the human and the divine"

[9] G. Bardy, *op. cit.*, IV, pp. 168–9.

in Christ.[10] For a man of his temperament devotion to one view meant that he was not indifferent to, but was plainly hostile to the other. In brief, then, from the beginning of his patriarchate, it became clear to everyone that Nestorius was importing Antiochean ideas into Constantinople.

The dispute

The struggle with Nestorianism began suddenly in 429 and, as in all the great doctrinal conflicts, the effect heretical teaching had on the piety of the ordinary Catholic faithful—incapable of understanding the significance of the finer intellectual differences of outlook and opinion, but at the same time endowed with an almost intuitive clear-sightedness in all that pertains to the purity of the faith—was to release an almost spontaneous reaction in defence of the faith which eventually resulted in the conciliar definitions of the Council of Ephesus.

What, then, happened at Constantinople? What did Nestorius actually preach? In the heat of the controversy idle accusations of all kinds were made against Nestorius of opinions he is not likely to have expressed: we can avoid, therefore, going too closely into details. The trouble began when, in the presence of the patriarch, a priest named Anastasius, who had come with Nestorius to Constantinople from his native Antioch, in a sermon distinguished the man Jesus from the Word who merely dwelt within him, and he drove his point home with the conclusion, "Let no one call Mary *Theotokos*, Mother of God; Mary is of the human race, and it is impossible that a human being should give birth to God". Nestorius refused to censure Anastasius, and declared he would himself refuse to call Mary *Theotokos*, or Mother of God. He recommended that both the expression Mary, Mother of God, and Mary the Mother of a mere man should be avoided, for both are capable of being misinterpreted. Nestorius said we ought to be content to proclaim Mary as the Mother of Christ.

[10] Hughes, *op. cit.*, p. 237. See Karl Adam, *op. cit.*, pp. 35–8.

Such a doctrine could not possibly pass unnoticed in any place given to theological discussions, least of all in one with numerous monasteries to keep the discussions going vigorously, as they would inevitably when it was noised abroad that the patriarch was importing new ideas about the Incarnate Word from Antioch which was regarded by the clergy and monks at Constantinople as supporting views savouring of heresy. In Constantinople the clergy and faithful rose to defend Mary's claim to the title, Mother of God. With his eyes ostensibly on his own monks in Egypt, only too liable to be affected by disturbances in monasteries in other parts of the world, St Cyril, the patriarch of Alexandria, was watching events at Constantinople. He wrote a long letter to the monks scattered all over Egypt in which he summarized the basic ideas of the doctrine of the Incarnate Word common to the Alexandrian theologians. Nestorius realized that Cyril was aiming at him in his letter to the Egyptian monks. After receiving two letters from Cyril, Nestorius replied to Cyril writing in a tone which showed that he was not prepared to retract, nor to compromise on what he taught and allowed others to teach. He recalled that thirty years previously one of his predecessors, St John Chrysostom, had been scandalously deposed by the notorious Council of the Oak Tree in 403. At this Council Cyril had been one of the most influential theological advisers in attendance on Theophilus, then patriarch of Alexandria, who had been appointed by the empress to judge the patriarch of Constantinople; he pointedly reminded Cyril that he had aided and abetted Theophilus in his conduct of the trial. Across the distance of time incidents like these may appear to be quite trivial, but they loomed large in the minds of patriarchs in those days, for they revived many of the bitter jealousies and political animosities of the past which had kept the three sees of Alexandria, Constantinople and Antioch at loggerheads for many years. It is necessary to try to visualize the quarrels we are about to describe in the actual human and political setting which converted them into the fearsome encounters they became, and to judge the conduct of the protagonists on both sides mindful of the pressure of the political circumstances in which they were placed. The manifest bluntness, whether unconscious and undeliberate, or intentional and premeditated, of St Cyril's conduct during the ensuing months may have contributed to the eventual vindication of the truth, but it must be admitted that at the time it seriously upset the harmonious relations between men whose responsibility it was as bishops to safeguard the unity of faith in the Church and avoid creating misunderstandings.

The theme of Nestorius' preachings about the Incarnate Word was not unknown to the Holy See. As already mentioned, the new patriarch had written to the pope to explain certain doubts he had in his mind, and St Celestine had entrusted the monk Cassian, the well-known author of Conferences to monks who later had to defend himself when charged with a secret sympathy for Pelagianism, with the work of making a thorough study of Nestorius' ideas. Having lived for many years in the East, he was an expert on oriental affairs and theological ideas. He wrote a report on the doctrine of Nestorius in which he declared his ideas unorthodox, and concluded by saying that they merited condemnation as heretical. Celestine, for his part, condemned Nestorius' theories at a Council held in Rome in 429, and on August 11th, 430 he wrote to Nestorius saying that he had commissioned St Cyril, who in the meantime had appealed to him as pope, to inform him that he was to obtain from Nestorius a retraction of all his errors. If he refused to submit within ten days Nestorius was to be suspended from his episcopal duties and deposed from his see.

On receiving the papal instructions Cyril took it upon himself to draw up a text of twelve anathemas or propositions condemning the new patriarch's errors to which Cyril demanded that Nestorius should submit.[11] The patriarch of Alexandria thought that by acting in this way he was but interpreting faithfully and exactly the mind of the pope direct-

[11] See Denzinger, 112–24.

ing that Nestorius must sign a profession of faith condemning his own errors. He was no doubt convinced that such a document could not be drawn up more satisfactorily by anyone than a Greek-speaking theologian acting for the pope. After all the present dispute did not concern the Western Church. The misfortune was that St Cyril saw reason to frame the twelve anathemas in a terminology that was Alexandrine, which rendered them suspect at least of Apollinarist tendencies by the adherents of the school of Antioch for the way they insisted on the unity of Person in Christ, and, as it seemed to them, on "the one nature of the God-Logos in the flesh".

While St Celestine and St Cyril had been conferring together, Nestorius had not remained inactive. Confronted at first with silence from Rome in response to his letter, and later with demands to submit to condemnation, as well as threats coming from Alexandria, the far-reaching imports of which he was fully aware, he sought protection from the Emperor Theodosius and persuaded him to call a Council at which he might have an opportunity to defend himself against Cyril. On November 19th, 430 messengers were dispatched to all the metropolitan bishops of the Eastern Empire inviting them to come to Ephesus for the feast of Pentecost in the following year to attend a General Council. The patriarch, confident of his own rights, never suspected that in successfully arranging this counter-move he was in fact preparing the way for the assembly which would condemn him more solemnly than even Cyril could have imagined at the time. He wrote also to the pope to announce the Council called by the emperor, and to say that he rejected the title of Mary, the Mother of God, not because he saw anything false in it, but only because he feared the consequences of its being interpreted in an Apollinarist sense. He said that he objected to the term *anthropotokos* (mother of the man) as too restricted in meaning. He preferred to use the term *Christotokos* (mother of Christ), for this alone seemed to him free of all ambiguity. But Rome had already stated her demands for a definite profession of faith in her doctrine, though strangely enough in the instructions he had given to St Cyril the pope had not stated precisely what the Roman doctrine about the Incarnate Word was, so evident did it seem at the time to the Church at large. He merely stated that the Catholic and apostolic doctrine is that which is accepted at Rome, Alexandria and throughout the Church, and that this is the doctrine to which Nestorius must subscribe to remain within the unity of the Church. In a letter he wrote to the emperor, Theodosius, the pope said that he agreed to the calling of the Council which he had seen fit to take upon himself, but he demanded—and the words were aimed at the patriarch now under the emperor's protection—"that no support should be given to those who claim to impoverish the Majesty of God to the measure of what human reason can understand". These words of the pope laid bare the hidden roots of Nestorius' errors, and gave warning to all the bishops of the dangers of a narrow rationalism threatening once again the purity of the faith.

The term *Theotokos* and its Latin equivalent *Mater Dei* had been in constant use in the Church since the time of Origen, that is, from about the middle of the third century, but it is difficult to date its first appearance accurately. Nestorius pretended to believe that its use had been confined to simple and uneducated people who were unable to understand the truths of faith and who, as a consequence, would not be in danger of accepting its theological implications. A theologian, on the other hand, could not but see the dangerous consequences inherent in the use of the expression. In fact, however, he must have known full well what the great and learned St Gregory Nazianzen had thought about the word *Theotokos*. As one of his letters shows, he did not hesitate to declare anathema those who would not acknowledge Mary as the "Mother of God".[12] No doubt there was some need to explain in what sense Mary is the Mother of God in view of the current confusion about the manner of the union of the two natures of Christ, but

[12] St Gregory Nazianzen, *Epistola ad Cledonium*, no. 1 (Epistola C 1).

Nestorius was seriously at fault in denying that Mary is the Mother of God.

The Council which Nestorius had been instrumental in convoking met under the sole authority of St Cyril, as "holding the place of Celestine, the very holy and sacred archbishop of the Church of the Romans". He is the first of the bishops named as attending the Council. The majority of the bishops who attended were from the East. We may wonder what might have transpired if a Western bishop of the intellectual stature of St Augustine of Hippo had been appointed to preside over its meetings. Perhaps the tactical abilities and practical efficiency of Cyril in coping with procedure and in enforcing his own way would have been tempered and shorn of their ruthlessness by the charity and theological poise of the great African doctor. But who knows? Would Nestorius, who in fact refused to appear before the Council when summoned, and who protested at having to stand before his accuser and judge in one and the same person, have accepted to appear before a Latin bishop whose authority and prestige were preeminent throughout the Catholic world? There is no harm in imagining that he might have done so, and that recent apologies for Nestorius, no matter how far-fetched some of them may be, are not purely verbal efforts of ingenious authors.

At all events, having borne with the delay in opening the Council for some time in the hope of the arrival of many bishops due to attend,[13] Cyril eventually pressed for the immediate calling of the first meeting and on June 21st announced that the Council would open on June 22nd, 431. Among the bishops who had not arrived for the opening were many of the supporters of Nestorius, including John, the patriarch of Antioch, and his party who, it seemed clear, were deliberately procrastinating so as to avoid having to take part in, or even witness, the condemnation of Nestorius to which they were probably resigned as inevitable. No doubt the impatience of the bishops who had arrived in time, together with the material

[13] The Council was due to start on June 7th, 431.

difficulties of one kind or another involved in providing for the many bishops attending a Council which it was feared might prove somewhat lengthy in any case, prompted Cyril to make the fateful decision of opening before the interested party from Antioch had arrived. On the day the Council opened it was clear that there would not be any deliberations about doctrine, as Cyril declared that the true doctrine had already been given by the pope himself for promulgation. The teaching of the Church was beyond the scope of any debate. The Council had been called in the first place solemnly to proclaim this teaching and thus to give evidence to all Christian people of the unanimity in faith of their pastors, and to obtain from the recalcitrant patriarch of Constantinople the profession of the faith that all accepted. On the first day of the Council were read the documents proclaiming the faith of the Church of Rome in letters written by Pope Celestine to Cyril and Nestorius together with the correspondence that had passed between Cyril and Nestorius, the evidence of the heterodox doctrine taught by Nestorius was heard, and finally texts from the Fathers and letters of the living authorities stating the unchanging doctrine of the Church opposed to Nestorius' theories were read. At the end of the day Nestorius was solemnly condemned and deposed by the vote of 197 bishops present who set their signatures to a document recording their sentence. Cyril wrote a letter to the faithful at Alexandria to report on the events of this momentous day. Written in glowing terms which have resounded down the centuries and are still mentioned by historians to the present day, it reads like the declaration of the sweeping victory that it is:

We were assembled to the number of about 200 bishops. All the people in the city remained in suspense from morning till evening, waiting for the judgement of the holy synod. When it was learned that the unfortunate patriarch had been deposed, all, with one voice, began to congratulate the holy synod, and to glorify God for the fall of the enemy of the faith. As we left the church we were led with torches to our dwelling places. In the evening the whole city was illuminated; women walked in front of us with perfumes of incense. The Lord has shown his omnipotence to those who blaspheme his name.[14]

The historian, looking back on these events across many centuries, can note dispassionately the blunders, and comment on the behaviour, of the protagonists. The extraordinary circumstances surrounding the opening of the Council puts into clear relief the most unfortunate traits in the characters of the disputants, which are the more regrettable when they appear as potent forces shaping the proceedings of a General Council. If love of the truth was one of the most conspicuous characteristics of St Cyril, the way in which he allowed his personal interests to influence him in drawing up his anathemas, and the ruthlessness of his antagonism to Nestorius, could have done nothing whatever to induce the unfortunate Nestorius to follow the painful path that his duty demanded. The very harshness of his treatment of Nestorius, however, serves to show in its own way how vivid and lively was Christian faith in the Incarnate Word and in the Mother of God in those days. The theologians discussed the most difficult problems of theology among themselves in technical terms, but the entire Church was at one in her allegiance to the dogmas St Cyril was defending. The term *Theotokos* expressed, in a simple and realistic manner, the Catholic doctrine of the Incarnation of the Word, and it is this simplicity and realism which are at the very core of the faith. Those for whom realities count more than the ideas we form of them could not possibly have set before them more vigorously the evidence of the realities the gift of faith makes known to us. Christ, the Word of God, is the Son of Mary; such is the teaching of the Church proclaimed at Ephesus. The entire Church accepted these dogmas no matter what difficulty human reason might experience in trying to conceive them. Thus, as was said above, Celestine put the whole Christological theology back on to its proper founda-

[14] St Cyril of Alexandria, Letter xxiv.

tions: the believer must beware lest he give support to the idea that "the majesty of God should be impoverished to the measure of what human reason can understand".

EUTYCHES AND THE COUNCIL OF CHALCEDON (451)

The formulas used by St Cyril in his twelve anathemas to state the truth about the mystery of the Incarnation were far from satisfying all the bishops. At Antioch the patriarch John and his group of disciples only reached an understanding with St Cyril in 433, and though John accepted Mary's title of Mother of God, "he nevertheless continued to teach an un-commingled union of divinity and humanity in Christ",[15] which was far too vague a statement about the union to satisfy Cyril's standards of theological exactitude. Cyril's victory, unfortunately, was not as complete as he had imagined. The followers of Nestorius went into hiding and endeavoured to pass unnoticed for the time being, but the predominant fear of the majority of the Eastern bishops was not the growth of Nestorianism: fear of a revival of Apollinarianism was their primary anxiety.

The anti-Nestorian movement had had powerful support from the monasteries, but now a heretical movement of monastic origin was about to break upon the world, and it was to win the support of hosts of monks as it developed into one of the most stubborn of heretical movements since Arianism. By an irony of fate the anathemas of St Cyril, the instrument that had contributed so much to the triumph of the faith at Ephesus, were to become the occasion of this new heresy, which was sprung on the Church after St Cyril's death in 444. The driving personality behind the heretical party was now to be the patriarch of Alexandria; the combined efforts of the party were soon to be directed to bludgeoning Flavian, the patriarch of Constantinople, and the entire Eastern Church to their support in the course of the outrage of the pseudo-Council of Ephesus

[15] See Karl Adam, *op. cit.*, pp. 38–40.

which Pope St Leo nicknamed "the robber Council". This new heresy is known as Monophysitism because it taught that in Christ there is only one nature (μόνος φύσις).[16]

Anyone who imagines that the monks in the East of these times resembled those we know nowadays in the West is profoundly mistaken. The monks of today in the Western Church bear only a remote resemblance to the monks of the East during the fourth and fifth centuries. Many of the latter were devoid of theological training and frequently displayed a kind of political zest to defend, often from mere bigotry, theological formulas popularized by an influential preacher which was in inverse proportion to their understanding of its meaning: their passions could be aroused in theological disputes to acts of violence curbed by little or no restraint, and at times they had been known to come from their monasteries and hermitages, in response to a preacher's summons, to make a mass demonstration in favour of his cause, overpower the civil guards, and even break into a patriarchal basilica! It has been stated that, during the upheaval at "the robber Council of Ephesus", certain monks went so far as to trample under foot the person of the patriarch of Constantinople, Flavian, who subsequently died of the injuries he had received. The attachment of certain monks and hermits to some personality and his theological formulas could become complete and unquestioning, and when the object of their blind hero-worship was one of their own company, whom they venerated for his austerity and venerable old age, the maintenance of order might present as many problems as the defence of orthodoxy itself.

The spread of Monophysitism was intimately associated with the person of a monk called Eutyches with whose preaching it originated, with the story of the intrigues in which he became entirely involved, and with an ambiguous kind of formula, reminiscent of that which St Cyril had borrowed from Apollinaris, describing Christ as "the one nature of the God-

---

[16] See Hughes, *op. cit.*, I, ch. 9.

Logos become man". St Cyril had written as follows in a letter to Nestorius:

> When we consider in our understanding the realities of which the one Son of God and Lord Jesus Christ is formed, we say that they are two natures; but after the union, as there is no separation of the natures, *we believe that the nature of the Son is one*, and that he is man and incarnate. If anyone says that he who is incarnate and made man is the Word of God, all suspicion of change is removed, for he remains what he was, and the union without confusion of natures is also professed by us.[17]

In using this kind of formula Cyril had in mind both the permanence of the Person of the Word, after as before the Incarnation, and the newness of his presence in the flesh taken from the Virgin Mary. In using the word "nature" he unfortunately gave ground for the Antiochean theologians to accuse him of the much dreaded Apollinarianism, but Cyril had been able to defend and explain his formula against all his accusers. He had been able to show that he used *nature* in this formula to mean what we shall call "person". But when St Cyril died and the interpretation of words like these was undertaken by a comparatively simple-minded person who was incapable of entering into the subtleties of his theology, it was inevitable that his doctrine about the union of two natures in the one Person of Christ would become seriously distorted.

Just before Eutyches began popularizing his version of St Cyril's doctrine, Proclus of Cyzicus, who in 434 had succeeded the aged Maximian as patriarch of Constantinople, had pointed out the ambiguity in the use of the word "nature" by many of the Greek-speaking theologians, and had introduced a new terminology, which from his time onwards the Greeks began to adopt. Proclus, replying to some Armenian messengers who had come to ask him questions both about Apollinarianism and Nestorianism, stated that the orthodox doctrine

[17] St Cyril, Letter XL.

of the Incarnation of the Word could be expressed concisely in the following propositions:

> We confess that the Divine Word, one of the Persons in the Trinity, was made man:
> We confess one *hypostasis* of the incarnate Word of God.

By using the word *hypostasis*, and speaking of *"one hypostasis* of the Incarnate Word" (in place of St Cyril's "one nature of the Incarnate Word"), Proclus showed clearly that he was in full agreement with St Cyril and all those who had defended the Virgin Mary's title, "Mother of God", and he also introduced an exceedingly useful clarification in the expressions of Cyril's own theology. Till this time the Greeks had used two words, φύσις, nature, and ὑπόστασις, hypostasis, to speak of a person. But they had invariably used the first term, nature, equivocally, and even the precise St Cyril had used it sometimes to mean person or self, and at other times to mean nature or essence; furthermore, they had used the word "nature" to mean sometimes essence in the abstract (manhood) and at other times essence in the concrete (human nature as realized in James or John). Proclus suggested that the term hypostasis should be used to denote a real individual self or person, and the term nature should be used to denote an essence, that is, what kind of reality an individual thing is. Thus hypostasis concerns "who"; nature or essence concerns "what". By adopting this usage the old ambiguous formula adopted by St Cyril "the one nature of the God-Logos become flesh", is changed to "the one hypostasis or person of the God-Logos become flesh"; had this change been made earlier, many of the misunderstandings which had bedevilled the discussions between the rival schools of Alexandria and Antioch might have been removed. Though this new terminology was adopted rapidly, the actual situation was so complex that there was no chance of confusion being removed instantaneously as though by magic. The Greeks, lovers of subtleties, warmed more than any Westerner can appreciate to the possibility of theological jousts; they could never let any change for the better take place quietly without a fray.

Eutyches was an ardent disciple of St Cyril. Cyril had evidently held him in esteem and had sent him a copy of the acts of the Council of Ephesus. He certainly prided himself on his knowledge of St Cyril's theology and work, but it is equally certain that he had little understanding either of the great doctor's thought or of the theological formulas associated with his name. He took his stand on the text of the famous anathemas, the wording of which Cyril had recast for the sake of making terms with John of Antioch, and of convincing the Antiocheans that his insistence on the unity of Christ's Person in no way impaired the reality of his two natures. Eutyches, however, was one of the many Alexandrian supporters of the saint who regretted this (so-called) compromise he had made for the purpose of making peace with John in 433, and who wished to defend Cyril now that he was dead by adhering literally to the text of the original formulas he had used against Nestorius. But he misinterpreted the meaning of these formulas so seriously as to say that in Cyril's doctrine Christ was not one in nature, or consubstantial, with us in his manhood. He held that the human nature that Christ took was absorbed into the divine nature in some way and so changed after the Word became flesh (or as the Word became flesh), because it was absorbed by the divine nature "like a drop of oil in the sea". Eutyches thus launched a new trend of theological opinion which reacted against Nestorianism in the direction of Apollinarianism in that it emphasized the reality of the divinity of Christ at the expense of his human nature. But it went far beyond the position of Apollinaris, who had at least accepted the reality of Christ's physical human nature, to the extreme limit of the oldest Christological heresy of Docetism, for Monophysitism denied that Christ's human nature *remained* a human nature once it had been united to the Word. He held, then, that Christ is one Person with one nature. In holding that the human nature was absorbed by the divine nature in such a way that Christ had only one nature, that of the incarnate God-Logos, Eutyches was in fact saying that Christ's human nature could only have been apparent. There were other problems. If Christ's human nature was not consubstantial with ours, how could it have been taken by the Word from the Virgin Mary, and how can we honour Mary as the Mother of God? If Christ did not owe anything to her as to his Mother, to whom did he owe the appearance of his human nature? Eutyches' answers to questions like these were confused. The least that could be said was that he was not clear in his own mind about the definitions of the Council of Ephesus. His confusion of thought was made quite plain when he appeared, after many summons and with the assurance of the patrician Florent, a friend of Theodosius who stood bail for him, before a synod held at Constantinople in 448 to try him. It was only possible to obtain a confused statement from him:

> I do not say that the body of the man became the body of God, but I speak of the human body of God, and I say that the Lord was made flesh of the Virgin. . . . I acknowledge that before the union of the divine and human natures, there were two natures, but after the union I do not recognize more than one.[18]

St Leo the Great taught, in the famous letter he sent to Flavian (known as the *Tome of Leo*, written 449) in which he condemned Eutyches, that it is not merely inexact, but positively incorrect to speak of two natures *before* the union, because the human nature Christ assumed did not exist before the Word was conceived as man. Before the Annunciation the Word alone existed as God. The bishops assembled at the synod of Constantinople had not noted this important point. Nonetheless, the synod under the direction of Flavian, the patriarch of Constantinople, stated the doctrine of the universal Church in a formula which is thoroughly Leonine in character: "after the Incarnation Christ had two natures in one hypostasis or person; there is one Christ, one Son and one Lord".

[18] See G. Bardy, *op. cit.*, IV, p. 216. Also Karl Adam, *op. cit.*, pp. 38–40.

The synod condemned Eutyches and deprived him of his dignity of archimandrite.

Eutyches was thoroughly out of his depth, but instead of submitting to the synod he persisted in his doctrine and took as his line of defence the astonishing plea that his formula, if not the same as, bore at least a remarkable resemblance to those of St Cyril so that he could not be in the wrong. He made a demonstration of being at one with St Cyril by appealing first of all to the pope, then to the protection of the new patriarch of Alexandria, Dioscorus, and finally, opening a programme of intrigues at the palace of the emperor to win support for his cause. The emperor, Theodosius II, befriended Eutyches, and as the final result of all his manœuvres the emperor decided to call another Council at Ephesus in August 449 and he appointed Dioscorus to act as supreme judge and arbiter. The pope, St Leo, met this emergency by sending three legates to preside at the Council, but when they appeared they were not allowed to read the letter, the famous *Tome*, St Leo had sent to Flavian, saying that Eutyches had been justly condemned at the synod of Constantinople. Dioscorus dictated how the deliberations of the Council were to be conducted, and enforced his will with threats of imperial sanctions against any bishop who opposed Eutyches. The imperial Praetorian guards were in attendance to see that Dioscorus had his way. The Council rehabilitated Eutyches, and condemned Flavian together with Eusebius of Dorylaeum, who had raised the opposition to Eutyches' heresy in the first place. When the meeting eventually became a tumult Eusebius and one of the papal legates, Hilary, managed to get away, and, after narrowly escaping capture, they eventually reached Rome to report what happened to Leo. The luckless Flavian was beaten up and dragged away from the altar to be trampled upon by the mob which probably included soldiers and monks. He died of his wounds three days later on his way to exile. Such, in brief, is the story of the famous "Robber Council of Ephesus".

At this crucial juncture in the course of events Theodosius died and in 450 he was succeeded by the devout Pulcheria, who later married Marcian. The empress immediately came to terms with the pope and they decided between them to rectify the disaster by putting the whole matter of the union of the two natures in Christ once more before the bishops assembled at another General Council. But St Leo only agreed to the Council as necessary for the sake of ensuring peace, and on condition that the truths of faith he had himself set forth in the *Tome* he had sent to be read at Ephesus, and the doctrine that had been stated at the synod of Constantinople, were accepted as beyond all doubt and not included on the agenda as requiring discussion. He appointed as legates three bishops and two priests: among the bishops was Julian of Cos, a Greek who had lived for a long time at Rome, and who was particularly well qualified to act as a mediator. Though convoked at first to meet at Nicea, the Council actually opened in the neighbourhood of Constantinople, at Chalcedon, on October 8th, 451.

Two sessions sufficed to clear Flavian of all the accusations of heresy that had been brought against him, and to expose the infamy of Dioscorus' conduct at the Robber Council. At the third session Dioscorus was convicted of abusing his authority and deposed. At the fourth the attention of the Fathers turned to the theology of the Incarnation, but, in accordance with the directives of the pope, there was no debate about the truths stated by him in his *Tome*. Paschasius, the papal legate who presided over the Council, declared: "The Council has as its rule of faith what has been defined at the Council of Nicea and what the 150 bishops assembled at the Council of Constantinople by the great Theodosius confirmed; it accepts the statement that Cyril made of the faith at Ephesus, and that which the venerable Leo, bishop of all the Churches, has given of it in his letter condemning the heresies of Nestorius and Eutyches. Such is the faith of this Council and such is the faith to which it binds itself without suppressing or adding anything."

All the bishops welcomed this declaration that the doctrine of Pope Leo was one with that of the earlier Councils and of St Cyril, and agreement was within sight of being reached when a number of bishops from Egypt, spurred on by their partisan allegiance to the memory of Cyril, raised the whole issue once again in a characteristically polemical manner. They stated that if the Council professed in the clear-cut way of Pope Leo's *Tome* the presence of two natures in Christ after the union, they feared a return of Nestorianism with a vengeance. They were, of course, grounding their fears on their own confusion in the use of the terms "nature-essence" and "nature-hypostasis or person". Quite understandably, the Latin bishops, whose terminology was more exact and whose outlook was more realistic, were by now exasperated by the anticipation of further wrangling on the part of a minority of Greek bishops. But this last-minute intervention only showed how necessary it was to find a formula of faith that all could accept. Thus a series of secret meetings and discussions was undertaken by a commission composed of the papal legates, six oriental bishops and several influential members of the group from Alexandria. Dioscorus himself was well and truly condemned, but it was necessary to win the support of the self-styled "Cyrillians" to a formula of faith, and above all to the teaching of St Leo contained in the *Tome*, which had clarified and done away with the ambiguities of Cyril's twelve anathemas. The formula of faith that was eventually adopted at this great Council marks a major step forward in the theology of the Incarnation in that it put an end to such one-sided interpretations of the doctrine of St Cyril as those embodied in the errors of Nestorius and Eutyches, and it stated the Catholic faith precisely and plainly.

The formula signed by 365 bishops present at the Council, in communion with the Holy See through the papal legates, stated:

> Therefore, following the holy Fathers, we all with one accord teach all men one and the same Son, our Lord Jesus Christ, at

once complete in Godhead and complete in manhood, truly
God and truly man, consisting also of a reasonable soul and
body; consubstantial with the Father as regards his Godhead,
and at the same time consubstantial with us as regards his manhood, like to us in all respects, apart from sin; as regards his
Godhead, begotten of the Father before the ages, but yet as
regards his manhood begotten, for us men and for our salvation, of the Virgin Mary, the Mother of God: one and the same
Christ, Son, Lord, Only-begotten, recognized in two natures,
without confusion, without change, without division, without
separation; the distinction of natures being in no way annulled
by the union, but rather the characteristics of each nature being
preserved and coming together to form one person and hypostasis, not as parted or separated into two persons, but one and
the same Son and only-begotten God the Word, Lord Jesus
Christ; even as the prophets from earliest times spoke of him,
and our Lord Jesus Christ himself taught us, and the creed of
the Fathers has handed down to us.[19]

This formula despite, or rather because of, its length left
nothing unconsidered nor hanging vaguely in the air. It gave a
precise and definite answer to all the difficulties which had been
raised during the past thirty years, and which had led so many
into the most lamentable errors. The crux of the mystery is
stated to be that in the one Person of Christ, the Word of God,
there are two natures which are radically different from each
other, the one uncreated and the other created. It is worth
noting that, on the question as to how these two natures are
united, the Council said nothing about the point St Leo had
made in his *Tome* condemning Eutyches, namely that of the
two natures one alone pre-existed, that of the Word. It was,
however, obviously important to insist that Christ's human
nature never existed on its own before it was assumed by the
Word, to safeguard the unity of Person in Christ. The Council
did this by saying that Christ is complete *in* two natures; it
avoided saying that he came to be *from* the uniting of the two.

[19] See Denzinger, 148 (for translation see Henry Bettenson, *Documents of the Christian Church*, p. 73).

The so-called "Cyrillians" were, however, not enthusiastic in their acceptance of this great formula; even after accepting it, they continued to voice certain difficulties and, as far as they were concerned, the peaceful settlement was, alas, something of a compromise. Three days later the Council disbanded after a final session to proclaim its faith and manifest its gratitude to God for the successful accomplishment of its work. The Fathers acclaimed the faith of all in the Incarnate Word of God, and its debt to the emperor and his wife. Christian tradition, however, for which emperors and empresses count for little in the making of conciliar decisions and definitions, has retained above all the memory of the saying ascribed to the assembly of the Fathers after they had heard the reading of the *Tome* hailing the doctrine of Leo: "Peter has spoken through the mouth of Leo: such is the faith." The beginning of the letter of homage that the bishops sent to the pope by the legates acknowledges his authority quite explicitly:

You have come to us: you have been for us the interpreter of the voice of Blessed Peter, and you have procured for all the blessing of his faith. We have been able to manifest the truth to the children of the Church in the communion of one and the same Spirit.

Thus the Catholic doctrine of the Incarnation has come down to us through the ages, and it comes immediately not so much from St Cyril the patriarch, as from St Leo the pope. However final the teaching of the Council of Chalcedon has been, it is sad to have to say that it achieved so much that a certain artificiality in the concluding peace settlement was almost unavoidable. The progress made by the Council is clear for us all to see today, but at the time it was far from being shared by all in the same fruitful manner, especially for some of the Greek-speaking theologians and Eastern Christians. Worst of all, Monophysitism was not dead: it survived the condemnation of Chalcedon, in particular in parts of Africa where the attachment to the terminology of St Cyril, still badly understood, blinded many to the progress that the theology of the Catholic

Church had made. In Palestine numbers of monks rallied to the support of Dioscorus and Eutyches almost as soon as the Council had finished. The widow of the Emperor Theodosius supported them, and before long there was bloodshed. But the history of these tragedies lies outside the scope of our work: we need do no more than point out how the battles of ideas and the clashes between theological schools had aroused the entire Church to defend the faith committed to her trust. Our task has been to show to what problems she had to attend in order to arrive at a theological statement or formula of the mystery of the Incarnation that would be sufficiently clear and precise to avoid all equivocation, and for the rest of time win the acceptance of people of all casts of mind and ways of thinking within the unity of one faith.

WESTERN THEOLOGY OF THE WORD INCARNATE

Catholic theology in the West benefited, as we have already noted, from the restraint and equanimity of the Latin temperament. The greatest of the Latin apologists of the second century, Tertullian, attacked Docetism with a forcefulness of expression which may at times surprise a modern reader. Certain formulas concerning the unity of the Person of Christ used in the Western Church were far from being beyond all reproach. For example, in writing about the union of the two natures of Christ, in the course of his treatise against Marcion, the Gnostic, Tertullian spoke of a "mixture" instead of a "union".[20] But he did at least explain that the reader should not take the term literally as he held that the two substances or natures remain distinct.

Since the thought of this great African writer influenced the theologians of the West for centuries, we give here a splendid quotation from his treatise *Against Praxeas* concerning the reality of Christ's two natures, and it will be noted that in

[20] Tertullian, *Adversus Marcionem*, 2. 27, "miscente in semetipso hominem et Deum".

writing about their "mixture" as in the treatise *Against
Marcion*, he explains his meaning clearly.

> He (Christ) must be understood to have "been made flesh" in
> this sense, namely by being made in flesh and manifested "and
> seen and handled" by means of flesh, because other considera-
> tions also demand that it should be understood in this way. For
> if the Word by a change in the form and a change in substance
> "became flesh", Jesus will then be one substance composed of
> two, flesh and spirit, a sort of mixture, like electrum made from
> gold and silver, and it begins to be neither gold (that is, spirit)
> nor silver (that is, flesh), since one element is interchanged with
> the other, and a sort of third substance is the result. Therefore
> Jesus will neither be God . . . nor man. . . . We see two natures,
> not mixed, but joined together in one person, God and Man,
> Jesus . . . and so unimpaired in the special quality of both
> natures, that on the one hand spirit carried out its own opera-
> tions in him—that is, deeds of power and works and signs—and
> on the other hand flesh experienced its own sufferings, "starving"
> in the devil's company, thirsting in the company of the Samari-
> tan woman, weeping for Lazarus, "anxious even unto death",
> and finally died. But if there were some third thing, a mixture
> of both, like electrum, no such clear proofs of two natures
> would show themselves, but on the one hand the spirit would
> have acted carnally, and on the other the flesh would have acted
> spiritually as the result of the change, or neither carnally nor
> spiritually, but after some third pattern, as the result of the
> mixture. . . . Learn, therefore, with Nicodemus that "what is
> born in flesh is flesh, and what is spirit is spirit". Neither does
> flesh become spirit, nor does spirit become flesh. But they can,
> to be sure, be present in one. Of these Jesus consisted as man,
> of flesh, as God, of spirit. In respect of that part which was
> spirit, the angel then declared him "Son of God", keeping for
> the flesh the name "Son of Man".[21]

After Tertullian St Hippolytus made a study of the different
activities of Christ, pointing out a diversity between them
which establishes the diversity of the two natures, and expressing his thought in accurate terms which were already in

[21] Tertullian, *Against Praxeas*, no. 27 (trans. by A. Souter, pp. 106–8).

advance of the later oriental theories about Christ's activities. Confusion in terminology was to give rise to two more heresies (in the East) concerning Christ's activities during the seventh century, Monothelitism and Monenergism,[22] both of which were a kind of revival of an implicit Monophysitism: by contrast the complete Latin theology of the Incarnation was already well grounded before the beginning of the fourth century. The key distinctions, which were universally accepted, can be presented diagrammatically as follows:

The One Christ, who is		Divine Nature		. . . Divine Activity
	{	and	{	Soul
The Person of the Word		Human Nature		and Human Activity
				Body

Just before the outbreak of the Nestorian controversy, the African bishops had made a firm stand against the errors of Apollinaris of Laodicea which had begun to infiltrate into Africa and to cause discussions about the permanence of the hypostatic union. The idea was being put around that when Jesus died on the cross the divine nature was separated from his body, and perhaps from his soul as well. A monk named Leporius was instrumental in popularizing this theory; he seems to have held that the buried body of Christ was not the body of God, and thus to have denied the permanence of the hypostatic union. Leporius retracted his errors with complete sincerity, and though one or two of the Latin Fathers inclined tentatively to Leporius' opinion, the majority had no difficulty in seeing that our Lord's dead body remained hypostatically united to the Word so that it was absolutely incorruptible. In brief, then, the Christology of the Western Church was remarkably free from ingenious subtleties, but it was precise in its use of technical terms and based on firm foundations. The confusion about the distinction between nature and person put to Pope Celestine, and the errors put around by Eutyches, left the Western Church completely unharmed. The *Tome* of St Leo

---

[22] See below ch. vi. Karl Adam, *op. cit.*, pp. 40–3.

to Flavian, which became the doctrine of Chalcedon, was rooted deeply in the tradition of Western theology going as far back as Tertullian. The Latin theologians of the years before Chalcedon did not, of course, use the term hypostatic union. But the sureness with which, for instance, the great St Augustine expressed his ideas about the union is remarkable, as we can see from the following extract from his *Enchiridion*:

> From the very moment that he began to be man, he was nothing else than the Son of God, the only Son of God, the Word was made flesh, and therefore he was God; so that just as each individual unites in one person a body and a rational soul, so Christ in one person united the Word and man.... For the Truth himself, who was the only-begotten of the Father, not by grace, but by nature, by grace took our humanity upon him, and so united it with his own person that he himself became also the Son of man.[23]

The Western Church never had to suffer the ordeal of grave crises in Christology from which the Eastern Church has scarcely ever been free since Nestorianism and Monophysitism have always had their adherents there. Perhaps this is because, as Abbot Vonier says so pleasantly, the Western and Eastern minds are sharply contrasted in this, that "it is more congenial to the Eastern mind to analyse its God than to analyse itself".[24]

The conflicts that were growing between the Roman Empire and the barbarians, which resulted in its invasion and destruction by the barbarians during the fifth century, were, apart from other contributory factors, external obstacles fatal to prolonged and serious theological reflection. Later, when the victory of the Catholic dynasties of the Carolingian era made an intellectual renaissance possible, the traditional teaching of the Church on the Incarnation, as expressed in the precise formula of the Council of Chalcedon, was firmly established in the Western Church. The theologians of the West avoided the troublesome sophistries which are often pleasing to brilliant

[23] St Augustine, *Enchiridion*, ch. 36 (trans. by M. Dodds).
[24] A. Vonier, *The Personality of Christ*, ch. xiv (*Complete Works*, I, p. 141).

thinkers and abundant in periods of high speculation, but which prove to be idle and positively harmful when employed in the study of the mysteries of faith. Once the struggles of the days of Feudalism began to pass, and as the great intellectual revival of the twelfth century ushered in the golden age of medieval culture which flourished till the end of the thirteenth century (in other words, from the time of St Anselm to that of St Thomas Aquinas and Scotus), Christology came once more into one of its golden periods, and became of capital importance in the work of theologians as it had been in the earlier times of the great Fathers. The masterpiece of scientific thought, the *Summa Theologica* of St Thomas, marks the highest achievement of medieval theology: nothing more comprehensive and systematic, nor more theologically precise has been written since, and theologians of all times have referred to the text of St Thomas as to the greatest human expression of the divine revelation contained in the Scriptures and Tradition. It is pointless to say anything about the *Summa Theologica* here; when we come to treat of the theology of the hypostatic union in the following chapter its ever-living value will become amply evident. This alone will show the reader something of the wonder of this work.

Before finishing this long and harrowing section, it may be as well to say a word for the benefit of those who have been scandalized at the extraordinary history of the battle of ideas which they have read in its barest outline, and appalled at the unsavoury incidents which are to be found associated with theological, and even Christological, disputes. The very fierceness of the battles bears witness to the firmness and liveliness of men's belief in Christ in those distant and strange times.

RATIONALIST PHILOSOPHY AND THE MYSTERY OF CHRIST

There is no possibility of our mustering even for a summary review all the doctrines which in the course of the last few centuries have been opposed to the Catholic faith in the mystery of Christ. It is one thing to expound a dogma of faith as we are trying to do in this book, and quite another to undertake an apologetic for the faith: we have no wish to confuse the two kinds of theological discipline. However, it is impossible to avoid devoting some part of our work, no matter how restricted it may be, to mentioning certain ideas about Christ of rationalist inspiration which are commonly accepted in the world today, even by certain Christians. Sometimes these ideas are put forward as deliberate or unconscious repetitions of attacks on, or gibes at the Person of Christ which have been borrowed from the works of certain pagans who attacked Christianity in its earliest years. At other times we meet with modern theories which reveal the utter inability of modern thinkers, imbued with philosophical theories of our own times, even to see the point of mystery of the God made man.

The pagan attack on Christ was most in evidence, of course, during the first three centuries of Christianity and the early apologists addressed themselves to the task of meeting it. Minucius Felix refuted the African rhetorician Fronto: Origen replied to the attacks of Celsus, and a number of Greek Fathers replied to the writings of Porphyry. It is very probable, and not just a curious legend, that Apollinaris of Laodicea was amongst the number of those who replied at length to views attributed to Porphyry. We know little, however, about the views of these ancient adversaries of Christ. What we do know comes from scattered fragments that have survived in quotations and allusions made by the apologists themselves. The political changes brought about by the Edict of Milan in 313 gave the Christian religion official recognition, and, apart from the persecution during the short reign of Julian the Apostate, guaranteed freedom to the Church to teach Christ publicly, proscribing not only those branded as heretics, but also the pagan enemies of the Church. In the days when the emperor himself called Councils and regarded himself as something like a lay patriarch, philosophers were no longer free to attack the name of Christ with impunity. Those who were of good faith were, indeed, able to express their opinions and doubts, but they wrote with respect requesting Christian theologians to enlighten them about the teaching of the Church, and not to deride Christ nor the Christian belief in Christ. Thus Volusianus wrote to St Augustine, not to deliver an attack, but to correspond with him about his difficulties and ideas.

In modern times many of the sarcasms and gibes of Celsus were reproduced in the eighteenth century by Voltaire, but the most infamous of all the attacks on Christ's Person is, perhaps, the work known as the Fables of *Toledoth Jeshu* which fully deserves to be stigmatized as "the lasting shame of anti-Christian Judaism".[25] Originating with the Jewish communities of the second and third centuries these legends from the Talmud, which fed the fires of the polemics of Celsus, were revived once more in Europe in the works of the philosopher Ferney and his disciples, who did much to foster the growth of the modern rationalist criticism of the teaching of the Church. The leaders of the Theosophical Society have not been ashamed to seek for the essentials of their so-called information about Jesus of Nazareth from this infamous source.

Socinianism

If we begin to search around for the root-source of the modern rationalist movement of thought about the Person of Christ—and, it must be remembered, to discover the source is not the same as to give an explanation, nor is the finding of a source a magical way of saving oneself the trouble of undertaking a refutation of the theories about Christ which are rife in the world today—we have to return to the Socinian movement of the sixteenth century. The Reformation prepared the way for the free discussion of the dogmas of the faith of later centuries for it rejected the idea of authoritative teaching as the foundation of faith. It must, however, be said that, though

[25] See L. de Grandmaison, S.J., *Jesus Christ*, II, ch. 3, p. 254 (trans. by Dom Basil Whelan, O.S.B.). Despite its age this famous work still remains one of the most reliable of many on matters of apologetics which concern Christology.

they favoured a theory of belief consonant with private judgement, the Reformers never anticipated that discussion would develop into the kind of free-thinking it soon became. Rationalism had secured a firm foothold during the Middle Ages in the University of Padua where Averroist theories of an absolutely independent reason, which came originally from Arab centres of learning, gained acceptance. These theories spread to other universities in Northern Italy at the time of the Renaissance, and it was from these universities, as well as some medieval Jewish quarters, that many anti-Christian ideas coming from the pagan writers of the second, third and fourth centuries found their way back into Europe. This anti-dogmatic rationalism infiltrated into France, Germany and gradually the whole of Europe from the humanist centres at Ferrara, Pavia and Padua. John Bodin, the jurist, in his *Colloquy of the Seven Wise Men*, summed up the objections that the new clientèle of rationalists of the sixteenth century were making against the doctrine of the Incarnation: "Christians and ignorant people may be persuaded to believe, but not philosophers, that an eternal God . . . stooped from such heights of perfection as to take to himself a body like ours, with flesh, blood, nerves, bones, and take a new form to expose himself to torture and a shameful death."[26] Bodin only showed his book to his closest friends but he had disciples and imitators, some reserved and others quite brazen. He even had disciples, who, disguised as Catholics obedient to the Church, worked by stealth from within to poison the minds of the faithful against the dogmas of the faith. Laelius Socinius, and his nephew Faustus, were among the victims of this campaign, and in their turn they were to become two of the most notorious innovators of anti-Christian theories. The Socinian sect was founded by Faustus, and though its numerical strength remained comparatively small, its influence was considerable, especially during the seventeenth and eighteenth centuries. It was from the Socinians that many of the philosophers of the eighteenth century drew

[26] See de Grandmaison, *op. cit.*, II, pp. 276–7.

the anti-Christian inspiration of their polemic against the Church.

The Socinians were the founders of Unitarian theology, that is, of the theology which rejects the whole mystery of the Blessed Trinity and regards God as being one person. Their theories about Jesus Christ follow from this basic article of their creed and philosophy, though it is certainly arguable that many Unitarians were led to reject the dogma of the Trinity, and to challenge everything that Christ said about three Persons in God, because they began by denying that Christ was God. In the Socinian catechism Christ is given a high position of dignity and even honour; in fact he is allowed to merit the apotheosis he is said to have received from the early Christians, particularly St Paul. Its basic contention was that Christ, whom the Church honours as God, "has not the nature of God, *because this is contrary to right reason*". "Right reason" is supposed to establish beyond all recall that "two essences whose attributes are contradictory to each other cannot be found united in one and the same person, for one and the same person cannot be mortal and immortal, having a beginning and yet be without beginning, be changing and yet be immutable. Furthermore, *two natures each of which is one person* [sic] cannot be united in one person, and if they are not one, but two persons, then we have not one, but two Christs".[27] Christ was only a man; if he had not been a real man he could not save us, nor give man the hope of his salvation. If he is called the Word by St John, this is because God chose to make him "his Word", that is, "the revelation of his will towards other men". But this Word still remains the man he was just like any of us whom he saves. St John said that the Word *was* flesh, not that the Word *became* flesh. The Greek word ἐγένετο does not refer to a becoming, but denotes an essence or kind of being a thing becomes. In any case, after his Ascension, the created Word sits at God's right hand and shares in God's power.

[27] L. Cristiani, article on "Socinianism" in the *Dictionnaire de Théologie Catholique*, col. 2326–34.

The Socinian approach to theology provides us with a very good example of the rationalist technique of reducing the mysteries of faith to the level of "right reason". The process of reduction consists in only admitting as true what conforms with "right reason", and reason is only considered to be "right" when it follows an empirical, scientific or historical method of investigation and analysis. Everything which surpasses the purely natural conditions of our life on earth, and so eludes for one reason or another our habitual standards of thought, is set aside as unscientific or irrational. The mysteries of faith, miracles, prophecies, mystical graces of prayer and the entire supernatural life of grace are all so many deviations from their acknowledged standards of truth which the rationalists have tried to expunge from their versions of Christ's life. They need nothing more to remove all that is divine and supernatural from the life of Christ, and on the basis of this method they made the mystery of Jesus of Nazareth vanish into thin air. Though they could not see anything superhuman in Jesus, they did at least regard him as having been a real man. Their theory that he became deified by being accepted by the Father as his Word was, however, little better than a concession to the mentality of the late sixteenth and early seventeenth centuries. The critics of the nineteenth century eliminated this last vestige of the supernatural and divine from the Person of Christ whom they regarded at best as being just a good man, and at worst as a sadly deluded idealist. Thus the Christ of the higher critics was not a teacher of truth, but merely a moralist exhorting sinful man to the "good life". Jesus was presented as being nothing more than "the revelation of the Will of God", and thence a kind of personification of moral values. Jesus came to teach man a way of life on earth, and the picture of Christ was cut to fit in with a purely human conception of "the good life". Finally, the confusion in the use of key words, which seem to have been left deliberately vague, has marked most of the modern studies of the life of Christ coming from rationalist writers. The confusion between "nature" and "person" in the statement of the Socinian position quoted above reminds us of the early confusions of the days of Nestorius and Eutyches. It may be an exaggeration, however, to say that the Socinians themselves deliberately misused these terms. The Nominalist philosophy which inspired their thinking cannot avoid confusions in dealing with ultimate issues in theology and metaphysics. The Socinian way of accepting the "divine" in Christ, while rejecting the dogma of the hypostatic union, was based on an utter confusion in the meaning of the word "divine" which has been exploited to the extreme by the modern critics.

As some critics of the contemporary Lutheran and Existentialist theologian, Rudolf Bultmann, have observed, there is no mid-way position between Catholic teaching in Christology and complete unbelief. Anything which appears to be a mid-way position is really only rhetorical wrapping or artful subterfuge.

As Fr de Grandmaison truly remarked, changes in the rationalist position, especially during the nineteenth and twentieth centuries, always kept pace with the stir caused by contemporary discoveries and changes in the natural sciences, "as if all that was new tended to disturb men's minds and cause them to question with anxiety all their earlier beliefs".[28] Thus, the liberal and modernist Christology of these centuries has been linked closely with the whole ferment of ideas about the meaning of history and the philosophy of history. The influence of Hegel has been extensive, but no less decisive has been that of the philologists and literary scholars who have lent a hand in the work of demolishing the sources of Christian theology. As we have noted, rationalist criticism in Germany was dominated by the figure of D. F. Strauss, whose *Life of Jesus* was widely studied, and by the theorists of liberal Protestantism of whom Ritschl, Schleiermacher and Adolf von Harnack are amongst the greatest.

Strauss was the pioneer and master: his method, which underwent slight modifications and alterations, remained

[28] See de Grandmaison, *op. cit.*, II, p. 288.

always basically the same with his disciples and successors. By a process of development which was initiated at the Renaissance, and which followed the Hegelian dialectical law of development, man had usurped the place of God so that for the critics Jesus of Nazareth became a symbol of deified humanity. "It is a humanity which is God made man, one in two natures, born of the visible mother and the invisible father, of nature and spirit. It is humanity that may be said to be sinless, to work miracles, and to die and rise again. All Strauss's efforts, therefore, are directed towards replacing the actual facts of the life of Jesus by what he terms the 'Gospel myth' . . . ideal conceptions subsequently translated in terms of history".[29] Strauss realized this objective in three stages:

(a) By selecting and setting on one side the actions, words and doctrines of Christ which he judged to be antecedently unbelievable and improbable;

(b) By eliminating incidents that he judged to be undesirable. He did this by showing their "mythical origin", and exposing them as wishful fulfilments of prophecies of the Old Testament.

(c) By justifying this sifting of the Gospels by his critical examination of the text.[30]

It can scarcely be said that any of the critics who came after Strauss attempted to accomplish anything more radical than this, and it is possible to detect, even in the work of the most recent of liberal Protestants, as for example R. Bultmann, the influence of these ideas and methods. The *Vie de Jésus* of the French critic, Ernest Renan, is just a brilliant reproduction of the work of the German master, and the ideas of the liberal Protestant, Sabatier, fit into the perspectives opened up by Adolf Von Harnack. The modernist ideas about Christ of Loisy and Tyrrell are substantially those of Renan and Sabatier.

There is no point in pursuing this line any further. We have no intention in any case of mixing theological disciplines here,

---

[29] de Grandmaison, *op. cit.*, II, pp. 293–4.
[30] See de Grandmaison, *op. cit.*, II, p. 294.

and of undertaking a detailed refutation of the rationalist position.[31] Our line of duty lies in expounding the Catholic doctrine of the Incarnation, and we have only touched on modern rationalist ideas for the sake of completing our survey of errors which attack the doctrine of the hypostatic union.

CONCLUSION

Jesus remains, and always will remain, the same. For the believer Jesus is the mystery of God revealed to man, a supreme reality before whom everything else in this world pales into insignificance. For the unbeliever and the rationalist he is a complete enigma. As M. Lucien Febvre said some time before his death:

Ultimately each exegete fashions a Jesus for himself, different from the Jesus of his fellow exegetes; but all the pictures constructed by different writers are alike in this, provided they avoid mere romancing—and Renan's *Life of Jesus* is an excellent example of a book which indulges in romance—whether they are to be found in large volumes or small books, they only represent what each writer has come to think "about Jesus"; they provide a surface account describing the events of Christ's life and a scientific study of apparently contradictory data which lead up to the unfathomable reality, the supreme mystery which to a mere man is little more than an imperceptible "something" hidden in obscurity.

A man accepts this "reality" by faith, or he does not accept it at all: there is no alternative between faith and unbelief.

Rationalism rejects everything which surpasses man's experience, or which is beyond his powers of reasoning, because for him, as for Protagoras of old, man is "the measure of all things". But in applying this principle in Christology the rationalist is begging the whole question of the mystery of

---

[31] Those interested in the Catholic apologetic for the Christ of Catholicism should consult L. de Grandmaison, *Jesus Christ* in three volumes, J. Guitton, *The Problem of Jesus*, H. Felder, *Christ and the Critics*, in two volumes; also J. Steinmann, *Biblical Criticism* in this series.

Christ. He is forced into an absurd position by his *a priori* method, and so long as he holds to it he is confronted with a hopeless dilemma. He has to conclude that Jesus is either an impostor, and then all that is associated with his name in the history of the Church, the thousands of martyrs who have died as heroically as they lived for Christ, and the countless millions of wise and learned men who have believed in him, together with all the saints, have to be set aside and the Church must be treated as one gigantic fraud which has defaced the history of the world for two thousand years; or he will have to conclude that Jesus is the Person he claimed to be, different from all others who have lived on the earth, whom Rousseau himself acknowledged as the greatest man who has ever lived on earth, and in whom Renan could not but recognize the clear marks of the greatest sanctity. If he accepts this form of the dilemma, he has to conclude that it is necessary to recognize Jesus Christ as God as well as man, and then he must abandon the principle that "man is the measure of all things". Rationalist thinkers incline now to one, and now to the other of these two alternatives, but they cannot avoid having to see the choice which ultimately lies before them. These two alternatives present themselves in varying guises.

The rationalist has to ask, on the one hand, how could a mere group of men possibly have been able to launch on the world a movement like the Catholic Church which has maintained itself in being and never failed to triumph over every threat to its continued existence, if its Founder is not Divine? And, on the other hand, how is it possible to reconcile the sanctity and veracity of Jesus Christ with the denial of that divine nature which he so persistently claimed for himself? Only faith in the mystery of Jesus, the God-Man, can remove these dilemmas. But this faith cannot be a mere proclamation or a blind unreasoning acceptance, for such an "act of faith" has no inwardness nor spiritual reality about it. It is not sufficient just to say "I believe in Jesus Christ" without understanding what one is professing to believe. Faith is an inward act of mind and will, which, in accepting Christ himself, seeks, not to explain him, but at least to think as best we can what we believe about him. We maintain the full vigour of our faith by keeping our minds and wills absorbed with the intellectual contemplation of the divine and human reality of Christ. Some accurate metaphysical thinking is required on the part of the theologian for this work, since it is only with the aid of a metaphysics that reason can enter into, and reflect on the inner meaning of, the great truths of faith, so far as this is possible to man on earth. The definitions of the Councils of the Church, and the theological work of the great doctors reflecting on the teaching of Christ's Church, are both directed to enable us to think the truths of faith and derive the greatest possible benefit from this intellectual activity. The removal of the ambiguities, with which confused thinking obscures as with so many clouds the mysteries we believe, is but a part of the life-work of the Church, whose Councils are concerned with presenting the teaching of Christ to us. In the next chapter we begin, under the guidance of the great doctor, St Thomas Aquinas, to reflect on, and make our own by thinking, the great truth about himself that Christ taught us, the mystery of the hypostatic union.

CHAPTER III

THE MYSTERY OF THE HYPOSTATIC UNION: THE THEOLOGICAL PRESENTATION OF THE MYSTERY

THE HYPOSTATIC UNION AND THE PERSON OF CHRIST

The purpose of all theological reflection and discussion is to clarify our ideas about the revealed mysteries of faith, to delve as far as we are able into the meaning of these mysteries by drawing out their various implications. Before entering upon any discussion or process of reflection, however, one point must be kept well in mind by everyone, and it is that, as the truths of faith are supernatural mysteries above reason's powers of insight, no one must imagine that he is being asked to find a purely rational explanation of, or to give a purely human account of, any truth of faith. Any such rationalist *tour-de-force* would only empty the mystery of its divine content, of its hidden reality, depth and supernatural excellence. The mysteries of faith are always of their very nature impenetrable to the scrutiny of the human mind. If Pascal's statement that God "alone speaks well of God" is true, theological elucidation of the mystery of the Incarnation revealed to us by God cannot add anything more perfect to improve on what St John, for example, has stated about the mystery in the Prologue to his Gospel, or on what he has recorded of our Lord's discourse after the Last Supper. In these, as in other passages from Scripture, we have God's own revelation about himself to which no man can add so much as an iota. We are not, then, about to try to prove the mystery of the hypostatic union by reason in the way that a mathematician proves the truth of his theorems; we have evidence enough from the previous chapter of the futility of seeking to account for the mystery by pure reason, and of the way all such efforts can only end tragically in heresy. We are not trying to improve on or add anything to divine revelation. We are just going to try to think as best we can the mystery that (in chapter I) we proved that God has revealed.

The technical terms used by the Councils of the Church in her definitions provide theologians with a universal language that is sufficiently clear and precise to help them avoid equivocation in interpreting the truths taught by Scripture and Tradition. These terms are intended for theologians of all ages, nationalities and ways of thinking to enable them to think, with that accuracy the faith itself demands, what God has said about himself, and what the Church believes about him. The theologian studies the teaching of the Councils of the Church that he may learn to think with the Church, and to think the truths of faith together with the Universal Church. Such terms as "nature" and "person", as they are used by the Church, have a meaning which is sufficiently clear cut to be understood by everyone, and they enable us to give an account of what God has revealed about himself by showing the internal consistency of the many aspects of the revealed truth contained in many different texts of Scripture and in the unwritten tradition of the Church. These terms derive their theological meaning, therefore, not from the human sciences nor from any system of philosophy, but from the revealed word of God which they serve to make clear to our minds. It may be true that certain philosophers use these terms in the context of their philosophical systems, but when the Church uses them in her official definitions she does not necessarily use them in the specialized senses in which a particular school of philosophers habitually uses them.

The Councils of the Church have no interest in imposing a particular philosophy, nor does she need the aid of the technical terms proper to a philosophical system to determine what Christ said. Conciliar and papal definitions of dogma only state what Christ taught with the degree of exactitude with which Christ taught so that we can understand clearly and exactly just what Christ meant us to understand. The language used by the Councils, even when they use such terms as "nature" and "person", or "matter" and "form", is a language which is within the reach of any thinking person who is thinking carefully about the mysteries of faith. It stops short of the technical refinements and elaborations of those terms made by philosophers on the one hand, but takes us beyond the often crude ambiguities of mere common sense on the other. There is even a certain flexibility about conciliar terms which makes their further elaboration by different schools of theology possible, and safeguards the dogmas of faith by enabling them to live in the minds of all Catholics of all ages, so that they can confront every kind of heresy which may arise and presume to sit in judgement on the word of God.

Hence to state the dogma of the Incarnation correctly and fully we use not only the words of Scripture (as in chapter I) in which it was revealed to us by God, but also the terms that have been given their proper theological meaning or shape by their traditional use by the Fathers and their actual presence in the Church's dogmatic definitions: we speak therefore of the defined dogma of the hypostatic union when we think of St John's words, "The Word was made flesh". When the theologians of the Middle Ages, and notably St Thomas, determined, in even more precise detail than the Councils of the

Church, the meaning of these theological terms "nature" and "person" with the aid of philosophical systems which they found or made acceptable for the purpose (Aristotelianism or Platonism), the originality of their work lay to a large extent in the fact that they produced an even more exact and precise account of Catholic teaching which the Church recommends to our most serious consideration without placing us under any obligation to accept the further refinements and elaborations they found reason to make. Theologians today, therefore, consult the great medieval theologians as recognized and authoritative guides who can still help us in our efforts to think the mysteries of faith ourselves, but we follow them without necessarily putting ourselves under any obligation to think just as they did. Some of the great theologians of the Middle Ages, and notably St Thomas, may have been philosophers as well as theologians, but in their theology they only used philosophy in a subsidiary manner, that is, they used reason, not to prove any theological mystery, but to examine the meaning of a revealed mystery as thoroughly as they could with the aid of their philosophy. We must say of these theologians what Fr Manteau-Bonamy has truly said about the definitions of the Church:

> The Church does not explain the Mystery of Christ in a philosophical manner; she only presents the Mystery to our minds in terms which are specially well-adapted for the purpose. The Mystery of the Incarnation was not defined at Ephesus and Chalcedon in the light of a reasoned philosophy of nature and person, but in the light of the teaching of Scripture and unchanging tradition. *There was no development of the doctrine, but only a necessary clarification in the ideas, used to express the doctrine*, to clear away existing equivocations and guide all Christians who wish to think about the faith they have in the Word Incarnate, their Saviour.[1]

This is exactly the work we are now about to undertake: we shall be using reason to clarify our ideas about God's own

---

[1] See *Initiation Théologique*, IV, p. 45 (italics ours).

revealed teaching, so that we may come to understand that it involves what the Church calls the hypostatic union. We are, of course, free to choose any doctor of the Church to help us in this work, but we propose to work under the guidance of the great doctor who has written most profoundly about it: St Thomas Aquinas.

Different Ways of Defining Personality

The present-day reader who is trying to find his bearings amid the network of ideas covered by a technical theological term in the vocabulary of St Thomas must begin by examining the ordinary theological meaning of the term in the first place. In theology a great deal depends not so much on the fact that a particular term is used in connection with a particular dogma, as on the way in which theologians are normally accustomed to use it. We have already seen, for example, how the word *flesh* conveyed spontaneously to the minds of the early Christians, familiar with biblical ways of expression, the complete human reality of the Word Incarnate. The definitions of the Church used other words corresponding in meaning to what the sacred writers meant by the word *flesh*, such as human nature, so that theologians speak of our Lord's human nature and not his flesh. We must now take the terms in which the dogma of the hypostatic union is revealed to us and examine their normal theological meaning.

In studying the theology of the Incarnation it is necessary to explain, especially for the sake of those who are familiar with modern philosophical terms and ideas, how the theologians of the Middle Ages approached the question "what is a person" so as to be able to understand the use they made of the term "person." The normal theological meaning of a term may *not* coincide with its "popular" meaning at any given time. Clearly the word "person" provides the key to our understanding of the mystery of the hypostatic union, and we must determine its normal meaning in theology.

Today the word "person" suggests numerous ideas, most of which belong either to psychology or to ethics. In the Middle Ages the word suggested ideas that are first and foremost metaphysical in character. Modern philosophy is less concerned with the permanent than with the dynamic elements which constitute personality and, as a result, certain aspects of the older ways of thinking about personality are unfamiliar to most people today.

How do people nowadays think of personality? Most modern philosophers, following the example of Descartes, Locke and Leibniz, define person as an actual awareness or consciousness of self. The fact of my thinking and the act of using my will enable me to perceive and to realize that I exist as the individual being I am. In being aware of my thinking, imagining and willing processes, I am conscious of myself as a dynamic agent. Personality is conscious experience of self. For Kant personality is constituted by free activity; for Renouvier by thinking and willing, for Ravaisson by the act of the will directed by reason. According to this way of thinking, personality denotes not a reality of the order of substance, but rather a "value", a prize to be attained and striven for by high endeavour. It is treated as belonging fundamentally to the order of psychology, and thus it is defined in terms of properties specific to our human nature, namely our will and our freedom, and to the moral or ethical order, so that it is identified especially with responsibility and character. Considered in this way personality could be defined as Guardini defines it on the basis of the observations we all have, that in acting on the world of our environment and in fashioning for ourselves "a world of our own", each of us has to exclude from "his own world" a great many of the things which exist in the universe. "The focal-point of this particular world is formed by the vital initiative thanks to which a man makes a place for himself within the whole world."[2] In other words, the more of an individualist

³ Guardini, *Monde et Personne*, p. 121.

a man becomes in his way of life, the more he becomes a person; thus a man's personality is the fruit of his interior activity of thinking, willing, planning and acting: it is something a man is aware of, something he can project on the outside world, something of the experimental order. In this way of thinking, personality is not considered in its ultimate depths, for it is not regarded as that which constitutes a man as the conscious individual being he is, or as a unique existent being having a certain autonomy and certain rights of its own. On this deeper, metaphysical level on which the medieval theologians considered personality, we can say that a person is an intelligent being who exists of himself, or who subsists, and because he is as a subsistent intelligent being he is the master of his own destiny which he has the right to settle freely for himself.

In thinking of a person as a subsistent, intellectual being the medieval scholastics went beyond the experimental level. They regarded a person as a kind of being, and personality as a perfection of being. Had they had them at hand, they would have been compelled in Christology to put the modern ideas about personality on one side as worse than useless. The application of a purely psychological or moral definition of personality to Christ would have led them straight into Nestorianism. To begin with, this modern empirical definition could not be applied to the Person of the Word of God; and if we say that we have a human person whenever we have a human consciousness with a human mind and will, there must be a human person as well as a divine Person in Christ. But the mystery of the hypostatic union means that Christ has a human mind and will, a purely human consciousness, but *no* human personality for his personality is that of the Word of God. There could not possibly be any union between the Word of God and a human person in a unity of one Person: a union of two persons can only give rise to a moral union between two people who remain two persons, and this was all that Nestorius envisaged Christ as being. In order to defend the unity of Person in

Christ while thinking of personality in a purely psychological manner, we would have to lapse into Apollinarianism and say that, as Christ lacked a human personality, he must have been without a human consciousness, mind and will, and that the Person of the Word supplied for their activities. Quite obviously, then, the medieval theologians were interested in the metaphysical analysis of personality, and the language in which they expressed their ideas about personality is quite different from that used by modern psychologists or moralists. They regarded a person or a self metaphysically, as an autonomous subject, that is, a self-existent being who has dominion over his own actions, so that the self is the ultimate centre to whom these actions are to be attributed: "he is a rational being with rights and responsibilities that can never be shifted on to someone else's shoulders. Personality means incommunicable appropriation for weal and for woe of one's deeds."[3] It is, indeed, this idea of personality that we must keep in mind when we are thinking of Christ's Person. Directly we apply this definition to Christ's human nature we find ourselves confronted with the whole mystery of the hypostatic union: the Word of God took to himself a complete and perfect human nature, and yet there was no human person in Christ "with rights and responsibilities that could not be shifted on to someone else's shoulders", for all the actions Christ did as man lay on the shoulders, not of a mere man, but on the Person of the Word (cf. Matt. 16. 14–16). The human actions of Christ belonged to, and are attributed to, the Person of the Word as their sole responsible agent. There was no human self in Christ to perform human actions, nor a human self to be regarded as responsible for these human actions. Thus the Councils of Ephesus and Chalcedon taught that Christ had no human personality: and the medieval theologians had to show that, though he had no human personality, Christ was nonetheless a complete and perfect man.

[3] A. Vonier, *op. cit.*, ch. v (I, p. 112).

SCHOLASTIC TERMINOLOGY

The Scholastics, like the ancient Greeks, viewed things in their being, and they considered the metaphysical structure of the beings we encounter in experience. The problem that was prominent during the Middle Ages, and that was really only a part of the long debate about universals, was concerned with the metaphysical status of natures or essences, that is, they debated whether essences are realities as such in their own right, or only realities as they are found in existent beings, or whether they are purely mental products of our thinking. For instance, is human nature, or the nature of this or that animal or plant, which we say we find exemplified in this or that particular man, animal and plant, also a reality as such in some super-order of reality other than the material one we know, as Plato envisaged their being found in his famous allegory of the Cave,[4] or are they not rather, as abstract and universal, just mental entities or states of the person who is thinking about some person, animal or plant?

Whatever the solution given to this question, exaggerated realism of the Platonists, moderate realism of Abelard and St Thomas, or nominalism of Occam, the thinkers of the early Middle Ages were in the habit of thinking about the abstract universal essence of a thing *separately*, or in abstraction from the real existent things of the world. Thus, they would consider human nature separately from this man John Smith, and that woman Mary Jones. Hence they would attribute to particular individual things the essences they were found to possess as if an essence was the basic property of a thing, which they considered as though it was distinct in some way from the subject possessing it. They would say, for example, that this individual person John Smith is a man, as though being a man was just John Smith's most conspicuous and characteristic property. They thought that we can know and state the characteristics which would make a nature a human nature, and those that

[4] See *The Republic*, Book VII.

would make a nature a pure animal nature: such statements or definitions were regarded as unchangeable and intrinsically necessary, each and all the characteristics of any one nature being required as a condition for that nature being what it is and no other. In the case of man, for example, the possession of a body and soul, complete with intellect, will and freedom were regarded as characteristics intrinsic to human nature as such.

Now, granted that we can think of it in abstraction from real things, the question arises as to how a nature, such as the nature of man, exists? The answer to this question given by St Thomas and the so-called school of moderate realists brings us to the idea of supposit. A supposit is a particular existent being which is, or exemplifies concretely, some nature of essence. Natures are not realities as such, as the exaggerated realists held, but only as realized in particular supposits. But why does a supposit exemplify or show forth many characteristic properties? Because *the many characteristics of a nature are variously realized within many different individuals or supposits*, and are attributed to those individuals by reason of their natures. A cat may be ginger, black or white: it is not gingerness, blackness nor whiteness. Each cat is the individual cat it is and no other, even if its colour is the same as that of other cats. The cat which I am now holding in my hands has a kind of individuality which endears it to me more than any other, it is my cat, and not just any cat.

A supposit is, then, a particular substance, a being in its particular, concrete individuality, which is of some nature or essence, and possesses various properties. We affirm all the properties a thing has, not to its nature, but to *it*, the individual thing. The permanence of the supposit amid the changes that go on in any being, and which make up its life history, enables it to survive these changes, and, in a way "support" them, so that we attribute these changes to it, even as we attribute the properties of its nature not to the nature, but to it. Inherence in a supposit accounts for the incommunicability of the accidental qualities of a thing, as well as the characteristics of the nature it exemplifies, for both belong to an individual being or supposit. Thus supposit is, in the last resort, an individual, or a being which exists of itself, so that it is incommunicable to any other being as a part of some whole.

Every natural individual existent thing is thus a supposit. If a supposit is endowed with mind and will it is an altogether special kind of supposit. The term "person" or "hypostasis" is reserved for a supposit which is endowed with a mind and will: such a supposit possesses rights which no other can possibly have. That which in a reasonable being is at the source of its knowing, both of other things and of itself, and of its willing, is the "Ego" or "Je" or "Ich", or "I", and this *metaphysical source and foundation* of a man's whole being is what the medieval theologians called *personality* or *hypostasis*. Hypostasis or person is thus the ultimate subject to which all the perfections and actions of a man are attributed. It is the "I" of the statement "I exist". As so conceived person is distinct both from the awareness a man has of his own self, and a man's moral consciousness which modern philosophers like to identify with his personality, for consciousness of any kind presupposes some ultimate subject who is conscious, and of whom he may be conscious. I may perform many actions of which I am not consciously aware, but those actions are nonetheless mine in some way. The "I" or self is more than and other than its mental states or free acts. A human person is a being who is autonomous for he is his own master and the master of his own actions, and a being who, because he is autonomous, does not and cannot belong to any other as an intrinsic part of its being. A person is responsible for his own actions, and these are attributed ultimately to him and not to his nature, even if his nature prompts him to do his actions. He is even able, if he wills, to defy God who created him and who keeps him and everything else in being. This mastery a person possesses over his own actions is, in fact, a reflection of the power and majesty of God. St Thomas truly said when writing about the divine *motio* acting on free creatures, that it is such as to make the personal acts of a free person *his own*.

In conclusion, we cannot do better than quote once more Abbot Vonier:

> The older philosophy takes personality to be something en-titatively static. The modern philosophers make it something practically all dynamic. The older philosophy has this advantage over her modern sisters, that she does one thing and omits not the other. She has that love of life which is the characteristic of dynamic philosophy. But underlying the transient phenomena of conscious life there are for the Schoolmen the stable elements from which life with its endless variations flows, and which give it continuity and oneness.[5]

The Use of the Terms Nature and Person in Christology

The brief analysis we have just made serves to show the normal meaning of these terms *nature* and *person* or *hypostasis* in the doctrine of the hypostatic union. Just as in the Trinity it is necessary to avoid confusing the three divine Persons amongst themselves, or with their divine nature, and equally avoid making the three Persons into three Gods each with its own nature, so in the Mystery of the Incarnation it is necessary to safeguard the unity of Person in Christ, as St Cyril was intent on doing, but at the same time allow fully for the reality of his two natures as well and the distinction between them, as the Antiochean theologians strove to do. The Greek Fathers experienced fully the difficulty of harmonizing the unity of Christ's being with the distinction of his natures: therein lies their great interest. Now if personality is defined as an autono-mous self or subject, there is nothing self-contradictory in the thought of one and the same nature belonging to many dif-ferent persons: thus we can at least see what we mean when we say that in God three Persons are one and the same nature.

Similarly in the doctrine of the Incarnation, if nature or essence is that which makes a being the kind of thing it is, and

[5] A. Vonier, *op. cit.*, ch. v (I, p. 115).

which we can conceive as belonging to an individual thing in some manner, there is nothing self-contradictory in saying that one and the same person possesses incommunicably two different natures, provided that, if the person concerned is a divine Person, the immutability of the divine Person and nature is in no way impaired. But clearly it would be absurd to say that a divine Person could assume into his own Personality a human *person*, for a person cannot assume, nor be assumed by, another person.

In saying this, have we explained the mystery of the Trinity or the hypostatic union? No. Because the manner in which the one divine nature belongs to, or rather is each of the divine Persons, or in which the Person of the Word assumes a second and a purely human nature, remains completely unknown to us. All we can do is show in each case that the mystery is intelligible and thinkable. We know the truth of the mystery by faith alone: reason can do no more than study the meaning of the mystery it knows by faith to be true. As the Orthodox theologian Bulgakov, says in full accord with Catholic theology: "The Incarnation remains a mystery for the human mind in that the immutable and eternal Being who transcends our powers of understanding unites to himself a changeable and temporal being which alone is knowable to us. The mystery lies in this union which surpasses the mind's power of understanding, for it is a mystery of the transcendent God Himself."[6]

But can we, by using these terms, show that various statements that we make about Christ, especially those which are in fact made about him in the Scriptures, and which appear on the surface to be mutually contradictory, are not really contradictory at all? For the Catholic theologian the answer is most decidedly: Yes! We are certainly about to rebut the accusation of absurdity or incoherence which cannot be avoided by the accounts of the mystery which the Church sets aside as heretical.

[6] Serge Bulgakov, *Le Verbe Incarné*, p. 124.

THE HYPOSTATIC UNION ITSELF

To realize that the Person of Christ must be divine, we have but to look closely at the meaning of two apparently contradictory statements of St John's Gospel: "Believe me, before ever Abraham came to be, I am" (8. 58), and the words of the Prologue: "The Word was made flesh" (1. 14). How do these two statements show that the eternity of God's Being in the Word is not incompatible with the newness, and the temporal character of his being as a man? These texts state in fact that the eternal Person of the Word became a man, but equally they state that in becoming a man the Word himself remained the divine Person of the Word. They state therefore that, as we say in the divine praises, Jesus Christ is the Word, and that Jesus Christ is true God and true man. Can we probe further into the mystery? We have seen that nature is not person, and that the Word assumed a human nature specifically the same as that which any ordinary human person possesses; furthermore, this assumption of a human nature by the Word brought about no change in the Word himself. The human nature of Christ is thus possessed by, and belongs to the Person of the Word, and there is no transformation in the nature he assumed precisely because the nature is in the Person of the Word, and not in the divine nature. A union of the human nature with the divine nature would have resulted in some transfiguration in the human nature (resulting from a "mixture" as of oil in water) such as that envisaged by Eutyches, but there is no reason why a union of the human nature with the divine Person should do so.

Our position is succinctly stated in a passage of St John Damascene which summarizes the whole effort of Eastern theology to present the mystery clearly:

An hypostasis *is* in the proper sense of the term. Hypostasis is that which subsists, or is independently. A nature which is assumed by an hypostasis and exists dependently on it is said to be hypostasized by this hypostasis. Thus the human nature of

Christ never subsisted for one moment of itself, and was never a natural hypostasis; it was hypostasized by the Word. It subsists, therefore, through the hypostasis of the Word by whom it was assumed. It is the divine Word which this human nature had and still has for its hypostasis. Hypostasis is taken here to mean the same as person.[7]

When St Thomas, as a young professor at Paris, was commenting on the *Sentences* of Peter Lombard—the text-book of theology in use in the medieval schools till the sixteenth century—he attempted to probe further into the mystery of the union of the human nature with the Person of the Word from the point of view of the actual act by which the Word took a human body and soul: in other words he considered the mystery in its becoming, *in fieri*, as the raising of the human nature to the supernatural level of the divine Person. It is certainly possible to avoid being misled by a deceptive use of words if we choose to view the mystery in this manner, provided due care is taken to explain that before being united to the Word the human nature Christ assumed did not exist. The Word did not raise up to himself an existing human nature, so there is no question of that nature having to lose its natural personality to give place to the divine personality of the Word. Later in his life St Thomas began to see that this way of thinking about the mystery is not without dangers of its own. After studying the theology of the Greek Fathers, and the problems they had to contend with, he revised his ideas about the way we ought to think of the hypostatic union. He wrote in the *Contra Gentes* (Book 4, chapter 28):

There have been those, like Ebion and Cerinthus, and later Paul of Samosata and Photius, who only acknowledged a human nature in Christ; they imagined that Christ was divine not by nature, but in virtue of a certain wonderful sharing in the divine glory which he merited by his works.

This position, however, . . . destroys the whole mystery of the Incarnation. For instead of teaching that God assumed a human

---

[7] St John Damascene, *Dialectica*; 43 and 44 (see P. Galtier, S.J., *De Verbo Incarnato et Redemptione*, p. 171).

nature that he might become a man, it teaches that a mere man became God. This, however, contradicts St John who said that "The Word became flesh", and not that "the flesh became the Word".

Similarly this position does not make any allowance for the descent and dispossession (*kenosis*) of the Son of God, but rather emphasizes the glorification and ascension of a man, and thus it contradicts the statement of St Paul who says that "He dispossessed himself and took the nature of a slave" (Phil. 2. 6), and only considers the exaltation of man to the level of God's glory of which St Paul later says "that is why God has exalted him to such a height".

Nor is the Lord's statement true on this view, namely that "I have come down from heaven" (John 6. 38), but only his later statement, namely "I am going up to him who is my Father" (John 20. 17). Scripture, however, conjoins the two statements: "No man has ever gone up to heaven; but there is one who has come down from heaven, the Son of Man, who dwells in heaven" (John 3. 13). . . . Again, "it was from the Father I came out, when I entered the world, and now I am leaving the world, and going on my way to the Father" (John 16. 28): in these two movements of descent and ascent both the divinity and the humanity of Christ are made manifest.

The key idea of St Thomas in the *Contra Gentes*, the idea which is at the heart of the later developments of his doctrine in the *Summa Theologica*, is that the pre-existent Word descends to take to himself a human nature. But the union of this human nature to the Word did not consist in the Word taking to himself a pre-existent reality, for a pre-existent human nature would be an hypostasis and thus incommunicable to any other being. Since hypostasis and nature are really distinct from each other, though in fact inseparable in the ordinary course of natural events, the Word could assume a complete human nature without any human personality of its own, or which had never actually existed as the nature of this or that man, provided that from the first instance of its becoming real it belonged to the pre-existent Word "as its owner" whose nature it would from then onwards never cease to be.

This human nature was complete *as a nature*: it only lacked
its autonomy and natural existence. The union is thus hypostatic or personal for the Person of the Word is the point of
contact uniting the divine and human natures in a unity of
being which is beyond any union known to man by experience. The theologian cannot explain the way in which God
brought this union about; but granted that God has brought
it about and revealed its existence to us, he can point out in
what way it is unique. Instead of beginning, therefore, with a
detailed analysis of each of the two natures considered separately from each other (or in abstraction) and then trying to
show something of the way God united them, St Thomas held
that the theologian ought rather to begin with the hypostatic
union itself and, emphasizing the unity of Christ's being,
analyse the different natures in Christ as they are found united
together in him. Thus in the *Summa Theologica* we find St
Thomas saying:

> In the mystery of the Incarnation the movement of descent
> of the divine fullness to the lowliness of our nature is of more
> account than the movement of elevation of man's nature to the
> being of God, for this movement presupposes that man's nature
> exists in some way. And this (union) explains why the human
> nature of Christ was perfect from the beginning of its existence
> (III, qu. 34. art. 1 ad 1).

The question as to how Christ's human nature is not lessened
or impoverished since it is without its own purely human personality scarcely arises with this approach to the mystery. So
far from suffering any loss, the human nature of Christ was
divinely enriched since it subsists, and has its being, in the in-
finitely wonderful Person of the Word (III, qu. 2 art. 2 ad 2).
The physical change of the flesh and blood of the Virgin Mary
into the flesh of Christ as well as the formation of his bodily
organs, the infusion of his human soul into the body, and the
assumption of the animated body by the Person of the Word
all took place instantaneously by the power of the Holy Spirit.
The great care that St Thomas took to seek for the correct

way of thinking the mystery of the hypostatic union may appear to some people nowadays merely a matter of formality or convention: provided we believe that there are two natures in Christ, what, it may be asked, is the point of discoursing at length on the manner of their union? A moment's thought, however, will show that St Thomas was fully justified in impressing upon us the superiority of his method of thinking about the hypostatic union. If we do not start by considering the real existent Christ, and keep him ever in our minds, we must begin by considering his two natures in abstraction, and then many people will find great difficulty in preventing themselves asking, at least imaginatively, how, before the Word was actually made man, the human nature he assumed was real, and how it did not suffer some loss from not having a human personality. Further, the central question with which we should be preoccupied is not that of God becoming man, but that of God being man: the problem is not about the hypostatic union coming about, but of the nature of the hypostatic union and of what the word "I" means for Christ. It was the Antiochean approach to the mystery from the separate consideration of the two natures which led Nestorius astray into thinking that Christ's human nature, being complete and perfect, must have been real on its own so that the Word might become a man, and thus have had its own human personality. St Thomas is, after all, only elaborating on the doctrine of St Cyril, St Leo and Chalcedon.

The theologians of the Middle Ages were fully alive to the possibility of our being deceived by an unrealistic use of the imagination and of language, and to exclude all dangers of error arising on these scores, as well as to prevent our embarking on more or less unintelligent ways of thinking the mystery, St Thomas insisted on adhering strictly to the principle that before the actual union of the Word to a human nature, there only existed the Person of the Word. Once the Word had taken to himself a human nature in the womb of the Virgin Mary, the being of this nature, its personality, was that of the Word who assumed it as his own, and therefore it belonged solely and exclusively to the Person of the Word. It is essential to avoid at all costs any idea of a "composition" or "mixture" of natures in Christ, and still more is it necessary to avoid any suggestion of such absurdities as a composite personality, or a duality of personalities.

Any such interpretation of the mystery is in flagrant contradiction to the fundamental message of the Scriptures that Christ is the Son of God and that his being is that of the Word of God. The mystery of the hypostatic union consists in the fact that the Word assumed a human nature into the unity of his divine being without impairing any of the properties of this human nature. Jesus said to the Pharisees, who were discussing his age and experience, with complete assurance and absolute firmness: "Before ever Abraham came to be, *I am*." The use of this expression "I am", with its reference to the Mosaic revelation of God's own name (Exod. 3), would have been understood by the Jews as implying that the Person of Jesus, the ultimate centre to which all the acts of Christ are to be referred, is God himself. The Pharisees certainly understood what Jesus meant, for, crying out that he blasphemed, they took up stones to cast at him.

A comparison from psychology may help clarify this very important point we are making about the correct method of thinking about the hypostatic union. A human person can be defined analytically as a being formed of a body and intellectual soul; this duality of body and soul suggests immediately that we might begin to study man first of all by considering each part, body and soul, on its own, and then later unite them together to see how these two radically different parts exist together in the composite unity of one person. If, however, we begin our study by working not from this kind of analytical definition, but from a description of an existent individual person as he is in the unity of his being, we shall observe that the diversity of his vegetative, sensitive and intellectual activities must be studied within the context of the unity of his being.

The unity of a human person's being is such that it is at one and the same time expressed by his intellectual, sensitive and vegetative activities. By basing our psychology on this primary certainty of experience, and considering a man as the real unity of his being, the problem of having to explain how the contrasting parts of body and soul (which one tends to think of as being independently real) came together just disappears as a pseudo-problem. A human person is a body-soul unit from the first instant of his conception. The principles of civil law which prevail at least in the West, and which give to a human being from the first moment of his conception the dignity of a person, accord with this exact philosophical conception which ought to be respected by psychologists in their ways of thinking about man. An exclusive use of the analytical method of study must inevitably give rise to pseudo problems about the moment at which animation of the body takes place or how we are to conceive the union of soul with a pre-existent organism.

Similarly St Thomas's method of studying the hypostatic union in the *Summa Theologica* enabled him to avoid the artificial problems of trying to explain the way the hypostatic union came about as though it was something made by God from pre-existent realities. Apart from simple illustrations to show that it involved no change in the Word he says next to nothing about how the union came about: "Suppose it should happen that Socrates, a real existent person, should acquire a hand, or a foot, or an eye, Socrates would not thereby acquire another being, but merely a new relation to these new members, because he would exist now not just with the aid of the members he had at first, but also with those he acquired later" (III, qu. 17, art. 2).

To put this in modern terminology we would say that if we take an organ from some living being (here, of course, the analogy is defective, because the human nature of Christ was not taken ready-made from any thing), and then transplant or engraft it on to some living person, the person who receives the engrafted member is not a different person, but remains the same person. The organs which are engrafted become assimilated to, and form a part of his being, just like those which were present before. They may be more healthy, but they will eventually share in the general vitality and being of the person to whom they now belong.

This comparison is used by St Thomas to illustrate how there is oneness of being, oneness of existence, and therefore oneness of age in Christ's Personality; though there be in him the human element, inserted at a given period of history into the vitalities of Divine Personality... that human organism that speaks, IS, exists, has being in virtue of the existence that is Eternity itself; just as the miraculously restored eye lives in virtue of the life of the older organism. For St Thomas, the conclusion that eternal existence is the existence of the nature formed in Mary's womb seems to offer no difficulties. He arrives at it as calmly as you arrive at the conclusion that you want food when you are hungry. Existence follows personality, he says; for ultimately it is only a personality that makes a rational nature exist. Now, Christ's human nature has Divine Personality; therefore it has Divine Existence. It is God, because it exists through God's existence.[8]

Today we need a theological language that is clear and unequivocal: in showing how the traditional language of the Church was gradually formed, and how in its deepest meaning it accords with the realities revealed to us by God, we have said as much as we need say for the time being. With this language of the universal Church guiding us, we are all able to appreciate something of the sublime mystery of the Incarnate Word, and approach God in faith through the human nature united hypostatically to the Word of God.

THE INTRICACIES OF LANGUAGE: THE RULES GOVERNING THE COMMUNICATION OF IDIOMS

If the only duty of the priest was to repeat, and the only need of the layman was to read the Scriptures *verbatim*, there would never be either heresies or errors arising from our own expres-

[8] A. Vonier, *op. cit.*, ch. viii (I, pp. 121–2).

sion of the faith that is in us. But directly we begin to comment on the Scriptures, to work out the implications of its teaching and show the consistency of its various parts, above all, when those whose duty it is to preach the Gospel face up to the demands this work imposes upon them, it becomes necessary to forgo the safety of sheltering under the texts of the Scriptures and face two dangers, first, those arising from our own thinking, and second, the snares involved in having to express difficult ideas in human language. Apollinaris, Nestorius and Eutyches were all victims of the traps which a preacher may easily make for himself in theology from his own ideas and vocabulary, and victims who at least before their condemnation may have been in good faith. They fell into heresy partly as a result of mismanaging their own vocabulary and ideas. Theology began to learn quite early in its long life the necessity of forming an accurate language of its own. Without the aid of such an instrument of correct thinking, the theologian is left to the mercy of everyday common-sense language, and then he will be for ever ill-equipped to deal with the finer points of theology. In the course of time theologians have worked out a set of rules to guide the way in which we speak about Christ. The rules, which belong exclusively to Christology, are known to theologians by a name which has an unmistakably archaic sound: they are the rules for the Communication of Idioms, or for the exchange of Properties.

An *idiom* is a special property or characteristic of a nature. Risibility, for example, is a property or "idiom" of man. The rules for the communication of properties guide the theologian in speaking about the different properties of each of Christ's two natures, and in affirming them of the Person of the Word to whom they belong. These rules are the outcome of the doctrine of the hypostatic union and they ensure that any statement we make about Christ either as God or man will accord with what we believe about the mystery. Nestorius had taught that in Christ there is a divine and a human self and that the characteristics or properties of both selves were to be kept firmly apart, for each self had its own nature. Thus he would not allow that the Virgin Mary is the Mother of the divine Self, the Word, but only of the human self whom he calls Christ. After the condemnation of Nestorius at the Council of Ephesus theologians began to study carefully the legitimacy of communicating the properties of Christ's two natures, and they came to see that communication is legitimate provided the properties of each nature are attributed to, or affirmed of the divine Person of the Word, and not to the other nature. We have had an excellent example of the Communication of Idioms before us for some time in the title of our Lady which the faithful of Constantinople defended against the attacks of Nestorius, that Mary is the Mother of God. Mary was the Mother of Christ as man, but as the human nature belongs to the Word of God, Mary's Son must be the Word himself, that is to say, the whole Christ of the hypostatic union. The whole system of the Communication of Idioms was elaborated fully by the scholastic theologians of the Middle Ages on foundations carefully laid by the Fathers. St Thomas devoted twelve articles of Quaestio 16 of the Third Part of the *Summa Theologica* to this very important matter.

Going back for a moment to the definitions of person, supposit and nature as they are used in Christology, we recall that person is the subsistent being with an intellectual or rational nature, endowed with all the properties of that nature (John Smith is a man and has a sense of humour). A nature is not a supposit, but is attributed to a supposit as to a subject. All the actions of a person belong to and are to be attributed to that person. The scholastics say: *Actiones sunt suppositorum*. But the activities of a person proceed from a person thanks to his nature, for a person acts according to the capacities of his nature which are manifested in some degree by his actions. A person cannot do any acts which lie outside or exceed the potentialities of his nature. Thus, Christ forgave sins, but only by the power of his divine nature; and he suffered from fatigue and was refreshed by sleep, but solely in virtue of his human nature. It is of the nature of man to live in a material universe in conditions of space and time; a man's activities must develop gradually in place and time. A man is born, lives and dies in some place, and everything he does is situated geographically and temporally.

God's nature, on the other hand, is transcendent, that is, it is above temporal and spatial conditions of being. God's being is eternal and unchanging: it is without "before" and "after"; God just is. Christ as God conserved the whole universe in existence, but as man he lived in Palestine for a number of years. The properties of a nature are peculiar to it, since they belong to that nature and no other; one nature cannot have the prerogatives of another without ceasing to be the nature it is. Matter cannot think, and mind cannot be extended. We cannot, then, attribute the properties of one nature to any other nature. This creates no difficulties so long as we are thinking about purely natural things; but when we come to think about Jesus Christ, who is one Person, we find that we have to attribute to him as to one Person and one subject of attribution the properties of two quite disparate natures. But we cannot attribute the properties of one nature to the other nature. We have to accept this as a necessary consequence of the doctrine of the hypostatic union. In principle these rules are clear enough, but at times we can find ourselves having to attribute such a diversity of properties and activities to Christ that we seem to be making contradictory statements almost in the same breath. For example, we have to say that Christ is the eternal, living God, and also that Christ died a miserable death on the cross. At times we can feel compelled to ask whether we are justified in making certain statements which easily come to our lips when we speak about him. St Thomas, for example, asks if we can say that "a man is God", or only "this man is God"? Are we correct in saying "God became a man", or, on the contrary, "a man became God"? The bare statement of propositions like these raises difficult questions, and sometimes it is not at all easy to decide which are correct, which are vague and which must be set aside as dangerous or heretical.

With faultless accuracy in his method of analysis St Thomas investigates all the possible meanings of statements like these, those which are Catholic, those which are false and heretical, and those which need to be clarified in order to express accurately the true doctrine of the hypostatic union. Thus, he explains, it is correct to say that "God is a man" inasmuch as the word *God* is understood to mean the divine Person of the Word. On the other hand, provided the reality of the two natures is admitted together with their union in the Person of the Word, the statement "a man is God" is equally true.[9] It is necessary to add, however, that in English we must use the indefinite articles with the word "man", and avoid saying "God is man" and "man is God". We often speak of "man" to mean "mankind": to translate *homo est Deus* just as "man is God" does not do justice to the argument traced by St Thomas in this article.

It would certainly be heretical to say that "a man has become God" for such a statement could only be interpreted as having a meaning in a Nestorian system of Christology. The statement "God became a man" needs to be used with caution as it can give rise to the idea that God underwent some kind of change in becoming a man. It must be understood to mean that a human nature was united to the pre-existent Person of the Son of God.

St Thomas gives the following rules for the Communicating of Idioms: (III, qu. 16, art. 5). The properties of both natures can be affirmed of Christ himself, and of all the particular titles (such as the Son of David) which we use to speak of Christ himself, provided the terms used for these properties are used concretely (not abstractly) to denote either both natures simultaneously: for example, "The Son of David" is Christ (the anointed one), the divine nature being the source

[9] See III, qu. 16, art. 2.

of the anointing, and the divine human nature being that which is anointed by being united hypostatically to the Person of the Word; or the divine nature alone: for example, "The son of David is the omnipotent Creator of the World"; or again, the human nature alone: for example, "The Son of God wept over Jerusalem".

Thus we can say correctly that Peter denied God three times, that Mary's infant Son enjoyed the Beatific Vision, that God has suffered, that this man on the cross is God, for in each case either the property of one nature, or something which happened to Christ in his human nature, or belonged necessarily to him by reason of his divine nature is attributed concretely to the divine Person of the Word, and not to his divine nature.

Billuart, the famous Dominican theologian, stated the rules even more tersely in the principle: *Concreta de concretis, sed non abstracta de abstractis*. In speaking of Christ we can always use concrete terms of the particular subject, but we can never affirm an abstract term of an abstract subject. We can affirm suffering and death of God, we can say that God hungered and thirsted, was sad and walked on the waters, for we are affirming concrete actions of the Person of the Word. But we cannot say that the Godhead or the Divinity was mortal, or passible, or itinerant.

These rules not only guide us in our thinking so that we can be sure that we are always expressing the mystery of the hypostatic union correctly, but they also help us to avoid any trace of the errors of Nestorianism and Monophysitism. A Nestorian would never say that God died, nor that God hungered or wept, because he would never say that God was a man: he would affirm all human qualities and actions of a human hypostasis, Christ the man. Similarly a Monophysite cannot affirm any purely human experience of God, for he would not say that Christ was consubstantial with ordinary men. It is only with the doctrine of the hypostatic union that we can affirm something human of a divine Person, and likewise affirm divine qualities of a man whom we adore and reverence because he is indeed God.

The liturgy, which expresses the great truths of the faith for us every time we celebrate the divine mysteries, speaks with masterly precision about our Lord and Saviour Jesus Christ. The priest who reads, for example, the office for the octave day of Christmas, the nun who reads her little office for the feast of Christmas, the faithful laity who recite attentively the prefaces for Christmas and the Epiphany should be able to recognize immediately the pure theology of the Incarnation in the very words the Church puts on their lips. We have a splendid example in the antiphon for the Office of our Lady at Christmas time: "A wonderful mystery is manifested today: a new relation of natures. God is made man. He remains what he was, and united to himself what he was not, without mixture or division." And when the faithful hear the celebrant at the Easter Vigil mark the Paschal Candle with the ancient formula:

Christ yesterday and today, the beginning and the end
Time belongs to him even as the ages . . .

they understand that this liturgical proclamation, like the saying of the apostles: "Jesus is the Lord", is just a transcription of the challenge that Jesus hurled at the Pharisees: "Before ever Abraham came to be, I am." The way of prayer is identical with the rule of faith: *Lex orandi, lex credendi*: the liturgy teaches us our dogma, but while doing so it nourishes our piety with pure theology. The Church thus teaches us the sacred art of choosing our words and shaping our language both when we are thinking about, and praying to God.

TABLE TO ILLUSTRATE THE CORRECT AND INCORRECT
COMMUNICATION OF IDIOMS

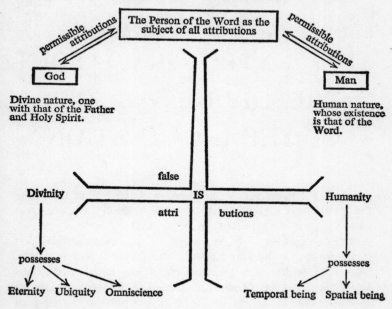

Rule: The attribution of an Idiom is only correct if it is made concretely of the divine Person of the Word. The attribution of one nature to another, or of the properties of one nature to another is incorrect. An abstract term can never be attributed to an abstract subject.

CHAPTER IV

THE CONTROVERSY ABOUT THE DIVINE PURPOSE OF THE INCARNATION

As we begin to reflect on the purpose of the Father in willing the Incarnation of the Word, we quite naturally ask ourselves whether, granted that Christ came on earth, as we know he did, in order to redeem us from sin and its consequences, and that in redeeming us he was fulfilling the Father's will perfectly, God also willed the Incarnation in any case, and apart altogether from man's sin. Did God will the Incarnation for its own sake, as an end in itself, or merely for the sake of redeeming man and restoring him to the privileged status of adopted sonship which he had shamefully lost? We all know that the one and only divine purpose for the Incarnation given in the Scriptures is our redemption from sin and death by the sacrifice and death of Christ on the cross. The Scriptures teach that in sending his Son into the world to die for us the Father manifested the wonder of his love for us: "God so loved the world, that he gave up his only-begotten Son, so that those who believe in him may not perish, but have eternal life" (John 3. 16). But would we be correct in thinking that a completely "gratuitous" and uncalled-for Incarnation, willed by God apart altogether from any considerations of man's needs, would redound to the glory of God more splendidly than an Incarnation willed simply for the purpose of rescuing man from sin?

Does it seem likely that the Incarnation was willed by God, as it were, contingently, that is, just to meet the situation brought about by the contingency of Adam's sin?

The famous Franciscan theologian Duns Scotus († 1308) considered that God decreed the Incarnation of the Word for its own sake and apart altogether from man's sin, for he willed that the Word Incarnate should be King of heaven and earth, the supreme Mediator between the Father and all created things. He questioned the adequacy of the view of St Thomas, that God only willed the Incarnation of the Word and the majesty of Christ as the supreme Mediator between the Father and all created beings merely as a means to rectify evil, or merely to redeem man from sin. He argued that the Father predestined Christ to glory "as the first born of many creatures" absolutely in his decree to create the world; the ultimate purpose for which God willed to create the universe must have been that the Word Incarnate should be glorified as the Lord of all created things. Thus, for Scotus, God willed to create man ultimately for the greater honour and glory of Christ himself: he did not will Christ to be man merely to redeem sinners. Scotus argued that if the Incarnation had been willed by the Father solely as a remedy against sin, or as an atonement for sin to the Father, God's supreme gift, the most excellent of all his works, the God-man, would be little more than a sort of by-product in his plan of creation, just "occasioned", as it were, by the chance perversity of man rebelling against God. In other words, a purely redemptive Incarnation would only be a kind of divine afterthought to remedy evil, and not the supreme purpose of God's creative plan. The glory of created things must necessarily be inferior to that of the Word Incarnate, so that God would not have willed the Incarnation of the Word merely for the sake of any good he wished to bestow on man. God must always will a good to men solely that he might in doing good to men glorify his Incarnate Word.[1] For Scotus, then, Christ is the centrepiece of

[1] See Scotus, *Reportata Parisiensia*, 3, dist. 7, qu. 3 and 4.

all created things, and the supreme purpose of creation as such; he is not just a means God "improvised to save fallen man from his own sins and the evils he had brought upon himself by his sins.

Scotus considered that he was defending a view that had the support of many early doctors of the Church, but in fact his theory was comparatively new for it originated in the Middle Ages, having been suggested by Honorius of Autun († 1152), who argued that sin, the greatest of evils, cannot have been the occasion for the Father willing the Incarnation itself, but only for the Father willing the death of the Incarnate Word as a satisfaction for sin. Scotus popularized and won acceptance for this view so that it has come to be known as the Franciscan view about the divine purpose of the Incarnation. Before Scotus' time it was favoured by the Franciscan Alexander of Hales, and the Dominican St Albert the Great, and it was taught later by the Franciscan missionary, St Bernardine of Siena. It was developed later by Denis the Carthusian, Suarez the Jesuit theologian, and particularly the great Bishop of Geneva, St Francis de Sales, with whose name it deserves to be particularly associated nowadays. The cardinal tenet of the Salesian theology is that the God-Man is at the centre of God's plan of creation, for God created man for the sake of Christ. The God-Man is, then, the starting point and the final purpose of all creation: simply speaking, God willed Christ and all things solely for Christ.[2]

The modern defenders of this view find support for these arguments from reason in the texts of Scripture, especially those of St Paul, in which the absolute sovereignty of Christ over all creatures is set forth. The captivity Epistles of St Paul contain a number of well-known expressions which, it is claimed, support the idea that God willed all created things solely for the glory of Christ. For example, in the Epistle to the Colossians we read: "He is the true likeness of the God we

[2] St Francis of Sales, *Treatise on the Love of God*, Book 2, ch. 4. See Michael Müller, *St Francis of Sales*, part 1, pp. 27–54.

cannot see; his is that first birth which precedes every act of creation. Yes, in him all created things took their being, heavenly and earthly, visible and invisible" (1. 15–17).

Against this Scotist-Salesian view, which has the support of many eminent theologians today, is what we may call the older view of those who link the Incarnation with Christ's redemptive mission, saying that the Word became a man simply to redeem us from sin. These theologians follow St Thomas[3] who discussed the problem on the principle that we can only know the purpose for which God ultimately willed a supernatural gift, especially such a unique gift as that of the Son becoming a man, from revelation, and therefore, we must abide by the clear teaching of Scripture. Now the Scriptures constantly and unfailingly teach that Christ in fact came on earth to save us from sin, and as no other reason is given St Thomas concluded that as far as we can know God willed the Incarnation as a divine means of atoning for man's sin, and not as the supreme end of created things irrespective altogether of Adam's sin. Christ came to die and merit the glory of being the Lord and Master of all things; Christ's pre-eminence is intrinsically bound up with his being the Redeemer. God did not create all things so that they might be subject to the God-Man. The Thomist view is undoubtedly easier to understand and to explain, and it lacks a certain imaginative appeal which the Scotist and Salesian view possesses. The view of St Francis de Sales no doubt appeals to many theologians because of the emphasis it puts on the gratuitous nature of God's greatest gift to man, and because it enables us to see more readily that God's creative plan was not "upset" in any way by man's sin.

St Bonaventure, the greatest of the medieval Franciscan Doctors, seems to have preferred the view St Thomas defended. St Thomas considered that we owe the Incarnation solely to the free act of God by which he willed to save man from sin, so that we cannot have any means of knowing whether he had decided to send his Son as man apart from what he has revealed

[3] *Summa Theologica*, III, qu. 1, art. 3.

to us. St Bonaventure said exactly the same: "Whatever depends on the will of God alone, and is in no way demanded by a creature, can only be known to us if revealed in Scripture by which the will of God has been made known to us"[4]; and he rejected the other view, which to him was an innovation, as anthropomorphic in character because allowing too much to a mere argument of convenience.

It seems that the supporters of the Scotist-Salesian view make the mistake of reading into the texts of St Paul on the sovereignty of Christ ideas which St Paul himself never envisaged. In the passages quoted St Paul is explaining that, as the Word of God, Christ is the exemplar of all created things, and that he created as one with the Father and the Holy Spirit. We cannot argue from what he says about God creating that he was writing about creation as such without considering either the possibility or the fact of Adam's sin: on the contrary the contexts show in every case that he is just stating what position Christ holds *in the present order of things*, which is one of creation followed by redemption. In the long exordium which precedes the text we have cited from the Epistle to the Colossians, as in that at the beginning of the Epistle to the Ephesians, St Paul is writing about the Christ who is our redeemer. In Ephesians, he says that the resurrection is the manifestation of God's will to exalt Christ above the angels, which proves that "God has put everything under his dominion" (1. 22); but we know that Christ merited the glory of his resurrection by his death.

It is very difficult to accept the claims of the Franciscan writer, Fr Chrysostome,[5] that the Scotist view can be found in the traditional teaching of the Fathers of the Church. Mgr Michel, in his article on the Incarnation to which we have referred, has sifted the texts of the Fathers put forward by Fr Chrysostome, and concluded that the patristic support

[4] St Bonaventure, *Commentary on the Sentences*, 3, dist. 1, art. 2, qu. 2.

[5] P. Chrysostome, O.F.M. Cap., *Le Motif de l'Incarnation et les principaux thomistes contemporains.*

claimed is far from being substantiated.[6] Many passages from the Fathers have to be misconstructed and wrenched from their contexts to make them serve even as favourable to the Scotist view. Texts, quoted to support the idea that God willed the Incarnation absolutely for its own sake, in fact treat of the equality of the Word with God the Father as two Persons of the Trinity. When Clement of Alexandria, Origen and St Ambrose comment on the scriptural theme that the Word is the eternal, subsistent Word equal to the Father, it is impossible to conclude from their commentaries on these texts that they must have been dealing with the will of the Father for the Incarnation of the Word, nor his purpose in willing to create the universe. It is equally false to conclude that because, in commenting on these texts, they do not always mention that Christ became a man to redeem sinners, the Fathers held that the Word would have become a man if Adam had never sinned. A point which is not mentioned by a writer because he is not dealing with it at all is not necessarily absent from his mind. In any case it is absolutely certain that all the Fathers held that the Word did become man to redeem us from sin.

To show that they always regarded the Incarnation and the Redemption as being inseparable we give these important extracts from the Fathers which are representative of the patristic teaching, hoping that those who find them of interest will consult the works from which they have been taken. First, then, St Athanasius (treatise on *The Incarnation of the Word of God*):

> For this purpose, then, the incorporeal and incorruptible and immaterial Word of God entered our world. In one sense, indeed, he was not far from it before, for no part of creation has ever been without him, who, while ever abiding in union with the Father, yet fills all things that are. But now he entered the world in a new way, stooping to our level in his love and self-revealing to us. He saw the reasonable race, the race of men that, like himself, expressed the Father's mind, wasting out of

[6] See col. 1495–1507.

existence, and death reigning over all in corruption. He saw that corruption held us all the closer, because it was the penalty for the transgression; he saw, too, how unthinkable it would be for the law to be repealed before it was fulfilled. He saw how unseemly it was that the very things of which he himself was the Artificer should be disappearing. He saw how that surpassing wickedness of men was mounting up against them; he saw also their universal liability to death. All this he saw and, pitying our race, moved with compassion for our limitation, unable to endure that death should have the mastery, rather than that his creatures should perish and the work of his Father for us men come to nought, he took to himself a body, a human body even as our own. . . .[7]

Secondly, we have the teaching of St Leo the Great as given in one of his sermons:

If man made to the image and likeness of God had preserved the honour of his nature; if, imposed on by the cunning of the devil, he had not brought upon himself the ravages of concupiscence from the law which had been imposed on him, the Creator of the world would not have been made a creature, the Eternal Being would not have been born in time, the Son of God, equal with the Father, would not have taken the form of a servant and the likeness of the flesh, but because by the envy of the devil, death has come on our earth and because human captivity could not be ended if God had not espoused our cause, he who, without loss to his majesty, became a man and alone was free from the contagion of sin, was offered up in the work of our redemption.[8]

Thirdly, St Leo in his *Tome* to Flavian, makes no mention of any purpose of God in becoming man other than that of restoring man from his fallen state of sin, of conquering death and destroying the power of the devil whose empire is that of death and sin: "This birth in time in no way detracted from, in no way added to, that divine and everlasting birth; but expended itself wholly in the work of restoring man, who had

[7] St Athanasius, *op. cit.*, ch. 1, sect. 8 (trans. quoted above, pp. 33–4).
[8] St Leo the Great, *Sermon* 70, ch. 2.

been deceived; so that it might both overcome death, and by its power 'destroy the devil who had the power of death'."[9]

The searching studies of Fr Bouëssé have made clear that in the mind of the Fathers of the Church the Incarnation and the Redemption of man were scarcely ever separated. St Irenaeus, Origen, St Athanasius, St Gregory Nazianzen, St John Chrysostom, St John Damascene, St Ambrose, St Augustine, St Cyril of Alexandria and St Gregory the Great are unanimous in seeing them together. Certain passages of Tertullian, Origen and Jerome seem to be rather hesitant or confused, but to take a few confused texts, and argue from them as from key texts that their authors held to the idea of an Incarnation without any need for a redemption of man from sin, is certainly to make these writers contradict what they clearly state in many other texts. Fr Bouëssé shows that what is clear in St Jerome, as in St Paul, is the link between the Mystery of the Incarnation and the redemption of the universe; what is not so clear is "the mystery before which St Paul is filled with wonder", that is to say "how the passion of the Saviour realizes God's plan for the universe, showing not merely what it effects on this earth, but what it also effects in heaven".[10]

It is interesting to ask how Duns Scotus came to envisage his idea of a separate Incarnation for its own sake. His theory was probably the logical consequence of his having followed a purely abstract way of thinking and reasoning in analysing the manner in which God acts. But in making his analysis Scotus failed to avoid the danger which besets us all of thinking of God in an anthropomorphic manner. When a man examines some course of activity, he is forced to analyse, and split up in his mind into separate parts, his motives for acting, the incentives which prompted him to act, and the various aspects of the end he hoped to achieve by his activity. This way of analysing activities is valid and necessary on the purely human level, and it forms an integral part of any study in psychology.

[9] St Leo, *Tome*, ch. 2.
[10] Bouëssé, *Le Sauveur du monde*, I, p. 295.

But it is invalid if it is applied vigorously to God whose activity and thinking are of a transcending simplicity. This is why St Thomas warns us that "God's understanding of a cause is not the cause of his understanding the effect, *for God just sees the effect in its cause*; in the same way, the willing of an end is not the cause of God willing the means. God only wills that the means should be ordered to the end. In other words, God wills that this should be for the sake of that, he does not will this because he wills that."[11] The way in which we have to think of the decision to act as being anterior to the act itself is one of the major difficulties we experience in trying to think of God's activity in the world, for we find difficulty in thinking of God, who is Being outside time, except as though he is and acts in some way in time. The analysis of God's activity into "moments" and into numerous "separate acts" of mind and will, some being for the sake of others, is no more valid if applied to God's willing to create or send his Son on earth as man, than it is if applied to the interior acts of God's life in the Trinity, that is, to the Generation of the Word and the Spiration of the Holy Spirit. Care has to be taken from the start to ensure that, in the analogies we use to think of the Persons in the Trinity, we are excluding all temporal relationships; the human terms we use to refer to the Father, Son and Holy Spirit will inevitably be meaningless if they are thought to imply temporal succession in God. The same is true if, in analysing God's purposes in willing the Incarnation of his Son, we think that God's willing of Christ's glory is the cause of his willing to create man.

Scotus was mistaken in treating Adam's sin as a kind of intrusion or misfortune which upset the first set of plans God had made for man's happiness. In creating Adam and Eve God knew that Adam would sin; he also knew that he had willed to redeem fallen man by the passion and death of his Son, and that by the obedience of his death he would merit the supreme glory for himself as the Lord of all things in heaven and earth.

[11] St Thomas Aquinas, *Summa Theologica*, I, qu. 19, art. 5.

God made a progressive revelation of his plan, but there was no progress in his plan. He gradually unfolded in a temporal sequence of different stages his one divine plan which we see realized as one long history. We should not lose sight of the absolute simplicity either of God's Being, or of the acts of his mind and will, for both his Being and his Activity transcend human being and activity. We must keep in mind the basic metaphysical principle that God does not know things, as we do, because they exist; on the contrary, things exist in the way they do, and are linked with each other as they are, because God knows them in the simplicity of his own Being.

Further, Scotus' theory that God wills the Incarnation of the Word just for its own sake as a good in itself that Christ may be the head of all creation, only makes sense if it is correct to think of God's will in the kind of way we think of our human acts of will. Scotus thought that, if Adam had never sinned, Christ would still have been predestined in the same way to be the Lord of all creation, for it is more perfect for him to have this title in a sinless order than to come to its possession as it were by chance, through man having fallen into sin. But Scotus forgets that the greatest of all Christ's titles is that of "Redeemer of the human race": in the present order Christ is far more gloriously the Lord of the universe, which he not only created as God but also redeemed as the Word Incarnate, than he would have been in a sinless order of things. Thus to say that man's sin was the foreseen occasion of God willing the Incarnation is not in any way to lessen the glory God willed to Christ as his own Son. All the works of God are a manifestation of his love. As God is love his works necessarily express his love for his creatures. Thus God did not need to will the Incarnation to express the reality of his love for us. We cannot use the old principle that "the good gives of its very self" to show that the only gift of God that God could wish as good or perfect in itself is the Incarnate Word, for outside himself God cannot will any effect as good or perfect in itself. The divine self-communication is only good and perfect in itself within the bosom of the Trinity. The self-communication of God in the hypostatic union cannot be perfected in itself for the limitations of a mortal thing, even Christ's human nature, impose limits on the created gifts God can make of himself to us.

There could be no gain in glory to the Word coming from creatures which could make his Incarnation as a creature a good to be willed by God for its own sake. On the contrary, an incarnation, even in a sinless human nature, would always be a "dispossession" of his own divine glory which could never be restored or "made up to God" by any limited finite glorification he received from creatures. God willed to create all creatures for himself in his own *divine* being. Scotus exaggerated in saying that man's sin was a kind of unfortunate chance event of man's early history, which he conceived as taking God, as it were, by surprise. God knew that sin was an intrinsic possibility to any created being, man or angel, because of its limitations, so it is not correct to talk as though, in the traditional view, God willed the Incarnation on the chance and almost unforeseen occasion of this unfortunate event taking place. Thus Scotus' way of looking at the Thomist doctrine shows up the anthropomorphic way of his thinking about God's will which St Thomas sedulously avoided. For St Thomas sinful man aspires for deliverance from sin and help from God, and God's will that the Word should be incarnate to save man shows that God willed the God-Man as a good which is perfect in relation to the work of redeeming man from his fallen condition. Christ has the supreme glory of being the Lord and Head of redeemed man, and thus Christ is the supreme manifestation of God to man in his actual state of sinfulness. But a God-Man would not be the highest manifestation of God possible to sinless man, for in fact God destined man to see God as he is in himself in the inner life of the Trinity.

God became man, therefore, to raise our earthly and purely worldly souls up to himself once more, so that in seeing Christ as man we might learn once more to know and love God himself. God's supreme love for man is shown in a King and Lord who has made himself the Shepherd seeking his lost sheep, in a God who has made himself a servant of all mankind so as to manifest the extremity and infinity of God's Love. If God did lower himself, and became a man just to save man from sin, it was in order finally to reign over all men the more closely and intimately as their Redeemer.

St Augustine expresses the need of man in his fallen condition, and the loving response to that need by God, in a beautiful sentence in one of his sermons quoted by St Thomas in the *Summa Theologica*: "We are only able to imitate and follow a man whom we have before our eyes, and yet it was necessary for us to follow God who is invisible, and not a mere man. In order, then, to give us an example we could safely follow, a visible example, God became a man."[12]

---

[12] St Augustine, *Sermon* 371, quoted by St Thomas in *Summa Theologica*, III, qu. 1, art. 2.

CHAPTER V

THE HUMAN NATURE OF THE WORD

An infant sleeps in a humble manger used by animals. Above him a mysterious choir of angels from heaven sings the glory of God. The shepherds and the wise men set out on their way in order to *adore*, that is, to worship this Infant as God himself, and to bow down before him as those do who are in the presence of God. God himself is here, but how is it that we find God with this sensitive body, and, yet more, encompassed by the humble necessities of a mere infant who will have to pass through the various stages of human growth and development? We can at least understand how those whose reverence and awe for the transcendent Majesty of the Almighty make them associate God with surroundings altogether different from these, have been sorely tempted to see in the events of Our Lord's childhood recorded in the Gospels nothing more than so many appearances. We can also understand how many who stood firm against the extreme heresy of Docetism were attracted by the idea of Arius, that after all this Infant who is worshipped as God is not really God himself, but only an exalted human being into whom the Word of God has somehow entered to manifest himself to us the more easily. Such an idea at least saves one from having to hold that this Infant really is God, or that God is really such a lowly human being. It is at least understandable that many who regard themselves as Christians and who venerate God sincerely still recoil before the Gospel account of the Infant Jesus by denying that he really is God himself.

The early Christian writers, mindful especially of the writings of St John and St Paul, reacted against those who attacked the Catholic belief in Jesus Christ by insisting on the pure truth of the Gospel narratives. With the theological good sense which comes to those who prostrate themselves before the truth of God's revelation, the early Christian people dissociated themselves entirely from dualist ways of thinking about the human body as an evil unworthy of God, which fascinated many who were attracted by certain Greek philosophies. What an absurdity for a disciple of Plato, convinced that the body is a shameful thing and nothing better than a prison-house for the soul from which a wise man has no option but to aspire to be freed, to be asked to believe in the God-Infant, wrapped in swaddling clothes and helplessly dependent on the protection of a mere woman! Volusianus expressed the revulsion of many pagan people of his time to the Gospel story of the Infant-God in a letter he wrote to St Augustine:

> How can it be that the sovereign Lord of the Universe has been enclosed within the womb of a virgin? . . . What? He who could not be contained within the universe lay hidden and gave forth cries from within the little body of a baby? He suffered all the weaknesses of youth, grew up, passed through adolescence, and acquired strength by degrees? The Lord of all things, he nonetheless remained far removed from his kingdom for a long time? The eternal King sleeps, eats, and experiences human afflictions like mere mortals: and no signs, no certain indications reveal his great glory and majesty.[1]

[1] See P.L. 33, 513, and St Augustine's reply in Letter 137, col. 515–25. In an interesting footnote Fr de Grandmaison mentions that Julian the Apostate wrote to the heresiarch, Photinus of Sirmium, who denied the reality of the Incarnation: "Thou at least art successful in saving appearances and in staying nigh to salvation, since thou hast rightly refused to admit that he whom thou considerest to be a god entered the womb of a mother" (Letter 99). Barely a generation later, Nicetas of Remesiana († 414) included in his *Te Deum*, among the litany of God's most glorious favours, the fact that "he did not abhor a virgin's womb". *Op. cit.*, II, p. 245, footnote 2.

These difficulties, which Volusianus of old brought up for
St Augustine to answer, occur to many people quite spontaneously to this day. Even practising Christians are sometimes
scandalized when they hear mention of the humble necessities
which our Lord experienced during his life on earth. Having
firmly pictured to themselves and reverenced their Saviour
haloed in glory, they find difficulty in visualizing him in the
conditions of helpless physical weakness he actually experienced during his lifetime on earth. In replying to Volusianus'
difficulty St Augustine made use of a simple example to help
him see more correctly the central mystery of the hypostatic
union. He put before him the mysterious union of the soul and
body in man. The soul is present in every part of the body it
animates: it is truly in the body, but nonetheless its powers
transcend its limits and reach out to all things. This is how
he argues: :

> What, then, is the soul itself, considered as something distinct
> from the bodily senses, without the mind by which it can ex-
> amine the marvels of the world? It is not by means of the senses
> that we judge the senses. . . . Do not harbour any fears, then, on
> God's behalf because of this little Infant's body, as if God must
> be compressed within it. God is great, but neither by mass nor
> extent: he is great by his power and his sanctity. God manifests
> his greatness in the smallest things; he is not little in that which
> looks little to our eyes. By his power, which he never limits in
> the most confined of spaces, he fecundated the womb of a Virgin
> who became his Mother; he united to himself in her a rational
> soul and through this a human body, taking thus a whole human
> nature to transform it for the better without suffering any loss
> himself, deigning to take the name of "man" to give man in
> return the gift of the name of God.[2]

St Athanasius writes in the same kind of way in a passage
of remarkable clarity:

> There is a paradox in this last statement which we must now
> examine. The Word was not hedged in by his body, nor did his

[2] See col. 518–19.

presence in the body prevent his being present elsewhere as well. When he moved his body he did not cease also to direct the universe by his mind and might. No. The marvellous truth is that being the Word, so far from being himself contained by anything, he actually contained all things himself.... Existing in a human body, to which he himself gives life, he is still Source of life to all the universe, present in every part of it, yet outside the whole; and he is revealed both through the works of his body and through his activity in the world. It is, indeed, the function of the soul to *behold* things that are outside the body, but it cannot energize or move them. A man cannot transport things from one place to another, for instance, by thinking about them; nor can you or I move the sun and the stars just by sitting at home and looking at them. With the Word of God in his human nature, however, it was otherwise. His body was for him not a limitation, but an instrument, so that he was both in it and in all things, and outside all things, resting in the Father alone.[3]

In these passages from the Fathers two principles are laid down which Catholic tradition has consistently upheld, and which were admirably thought out later in their various implications by St Thomas. The first is that the Word of God is united to a human nature as intimately as the soul is united to the body in man. The union of the divine and human natures is effected in the Person of the Word, as the very expression "hypostatic union" reminds us. As in a man the body lives dependently on the soul which informs it, so Christ's human nature exists dependently on (though it is not informed by) the Person of the Word of God, and his human nature shares the existence proper to the Person of the Word. But whereas the human body is a limitation to the soul which informs the body, Christ's human nature is no limitation at all to God who assumed it. The second principle concerns the scope or range of human qualities assumed by the Word in becoming man: it is that nothing that is human, or that can

[3] St Athanasius, *op. cit.*, ch. 3, sect. 17 (trans. quoted above).

be envisaged as contributing to man's salvation—in other
words nothing that is of the flesh or proper to man's nature—
is incompatible with the dignity of God. In becoming man, and
taking our flesh to himself, God suffered no loss of any kind,
but he raised up to the divine level everything in man save only
sin and our sinful inclinations. It was necessary that Christ
should really experience the ordinary and even the humble
things of human life so as to be a man like to each of us, and
thus sanctify the ordinary things of human life. As the Church
sings at Lauds on Christmas Day,

> Blest author of this earthy frame,
> To take a servant's form he came,
> That, cloth'd in flesh and flesh to aid,
> He might not lose what he had made.[4]

Do we not find the Scriptures laying down these principles
in unmistakably clear terms? The texts of St Paul are known
to all those who have celebrated the feasts of Christmas and
Easter for many years. One of the most striking texts is from
the Epistle to the Philippians: "His nature is, from the first,
divine, and yet he did not see, in the rank of Godhead, a prize
to be coveted; he dispossessed himself, and took the nature of
a slave, fashioned in the likeness of men, and presenting himself to us in human form" (Phil. 2. 6–7).

The words "in the likeness of" are not a sufficiently forceful
translation of the Greek ἐν ὁμοιώματι to convey the whole of
St Paul's meaning. He means that Christ became exactly equal
with us men in an identity of nature. St Paul is saying that as
God Christ is consubstantial with the Father—we venerate this
oneness of nature between Christ and the Father every Sunday
as we sing the Creed at Mass—and that in his human nature
Christ is consubstantial with us men.

The Epistle to the Hebrews, which expresses the thought of
the Apostle on the qualities of Christ as the Mediator between

---

[4] Benedictine Vesperal, p. 114.

God and men, explains the full extent of the Incarnation in similar terms:

> After all, he does not make himself the angel's champion, no sign of that; it is the sons of Abraham that he champions. And so he must needs become altogether like his brethren [ὁμοιωθῆναι]. He would be a high priest who could feel for us and be our representative before God, to make atonement for the sins of the people. It is because he himself has been tried by suffering that he has power to help us in the trials we undergo (Heb. 2. 16–18).

THE WEAKNESSES AND INFIRMITIES OF THE BODY OF CHRIST

The interpretation put on the passage quoted above from Philippians, in which St Paul says that the Word "dispossessed" or "emptied" (ἐκένωσεν), is well known: the supporters of the so-called "kenosis theory" held that in "dispossessing" himself Christ suffered a real degradation or loss to his divine nature. In fact, however, the Greek word for "dispossessed" only means that in becoming a man a certain unseemliness or unsightliness affected the Word of God. St Paul is saying, then, that the Word put aside his divine glory, not because he suffered any loss to his divine nature in becoming a man, but because he appeared on earth as a poor and humble man. Though Christ was God, he did not appear outwardly in the splendour of his divinity. The Son of God "dispossessed" himself in the sense that he appeared to be less than he really was, a mere man, for he concealed from our sight the glories of his divinity. Christ appeared to men as a slave or humble servant. What kind of bodily appearance did he have? In more detail what weakness of body must we exclude from the long list of human weaknesses as necessarily incompatible with his divine nature? This question comes naturally to the mind of any Catholic who realizes without difficulty that Christ could not have suffered any human weaknesses or infirmities that would have been either a degradation to his sacred Person, or an

obstacle rather than a means to our redemption. The solutions
offered to this question by some of the Fathers were at times
rather varied and inconsistent. However, the truly profound
insight into the principles by which St Thomas was later
guided in dealing with many of the intricate details involved
in this question is by no means lacking from the writings of
many of the Fathers. Despite a certain hesitancy in developing
his ideas, St Hilary of Poitiers is of special interest for what
he has to say, which is to the effect that

> if Jesus suffered, if he hungered and thirsted, if he groaned and
> wept, it was because he freely willed to do so, either because
> he accepted once and for all the divine ordinance, that despite
> his divine prerogatives, his human nature should be subject to
> the laws which are common to all men, or because he freely
> chose, by repeated acts of the will renewed unceasingly through-
> out his life, to lay aside the privileges to which he was really
> entitled as man. . . . The sufferings and weaknesses of Christ,
> so far from providing us with an argument against his being
> God, are, on the contrary, a proof of it, for *they are effects of
> his own divine power.*[5]

The real insight of St Hilary into the question comes to light
in the final words of this passage which we have italicized, for,
as Fr Bouëssé says, in these few words "the affirmation of the
sovereign Majesty of the Word over his assumed nature" is
most vividly emphasized.[6] St Hilary realized that, if God willed
to be a man like unto us in his human nature, the Word would
necessarily have to take upon himself the weaknesses and infirmities which are intrinsically connected with our normal
human lives on earth. No one can say that the natural weaknesses of the body experienced by ordinary men in the ordinary
works of daily life are of themselves an extra or undue humilia-
tion to a man. Such infirmities would not of themselves be
incompatible with God's Majesty, so long as God willed to be
a man like other men. But as he could have become a man,

[5] St Hilary, *On the Trinity*, Book x, 14, 48 and 68.
[6] Bouëssé, *Le Sauveur du monde*, II, p. 447.

and yet have exempted himself from living in lowly, humble human conditions, the Word took upon himself of his own free will the humble conditions of human nature with its co-natural human weaknesses, so that he might use them by his divine power to accomplish a divine work, that of our redemption. It was in the accomplishment of this work that the divine omnipotence would shine through all his bodily infirmities. But we must exclude as incompatible with the dignity and sanctity of the Word of God all infirmities which are not intrinsic to human nature as God made it; they are rather degradations of our nature which involve disorder in the use we make of ourselves and our bodily members. These defects are due directly to original sin, and are not inherent in our nature as God himself made it. Christ could not, then, be subject to disorders of this kind, for God and sin, as well as any sinful inclination, are incompatible. Christ came not to accept sin, but to conquer it. He only accepted a human body like ours that he might conquer sin in it and so raise our own bodies above everything that is sinful in them.

St Thomas developed the teaching of St Hilary very considerably. Having shown that Christ had no bodily defects which are immediately connected with sin itself, he pointed out that Christ's body was conceived by the Holy Spirit, who being infinite in power and wisdom, cannot fail nor err. True Christ's body was made directly by God. During his life Christ committed no evil in the ordering of his life according to the will of his Father, and so he could not have brought any harm upon his body as Adam did. But there are defects of the body which, though they have been incurred by all men by reason of the sin of our first parents, are none the less perfectly natural in themselves; such, for example, are death resulting from wounds inflicted by another, bodily fatigue, hunger, thirst and the like. Christ accepted all these infirmities which St John Damascene aptly called "natural but indetractible passions". They are natural because they pertain to man as man and not as sinful, even if God only permitted them as a punishment for sin, and they are indetractible because they do not imply any defect of soul or of divine grace.[7] St Thomas allows that Christ could take upon himself those bodily defects which we in fact suffer as a punishment for sin, but which are of themselves natural defects (for example, hunger, thirst, fatigue, etc.), but, he argues, Christ could not have suffered any bodily disorder or any defects which issue from some internal disorder (for example, the possibility of death from disease, or any intrinsic corruption). Christ assumed our purely natural infirmities so that by their means and in our own nature he might deliver us from sin. Thus Christ could be done to death, but he could not die a physical death as the result of disease. He could suffer hunger and thirst, grow tired and feel sad, but he could not suffer from any organic disease that would cause him suffering of some personal kind and expose him to the certainty of death by so-called "natural causes". The infirmities of Christ's body, then, could not bring him any purely personal harm, for he did not suffer from any purely personal infirmities, least of all from disease, concupiscence or natural corruption which are immediately connected with man's status as a sinner before God. Such infirmities would have been incompatible with the sanctity of his Person. But the Word did take upon himself the infirmities which are purely natural and common properties of our human nature. Thus Abbot Vonier wrote: "The ruling principle is the raising up of the human race through the Incarnation. Only such infirmities were to be assumed which were co-extensive with the race itself, and whose healing therefore in Christ would affect the healing of the whole race. Infirmities that come from individual causes, not universal racial causes, Christ had not to take upon himself."[8]

[7] St Thomas, *Summa Theologica*, III, qu. 14, art. 4. Adam was preserved from these infirmities of nature by the special favour of God who endowed him with the preternatural gifts he lost by his sin together with sanctifying grace. For St John Damascene, see *De Fide Orthodoxa*, I, ch. 14; III, ch. 20. (*P.G.* 94, 859: 1082).

[8] A. Vonier, *op. cit.*, ch. xx (I, p. 166).

St Augustine wrote with rare delicacy of feeling about the bodily infirmities of Christ in one of his homilies on the Gospel of St John. One cannot read the text without feeling something of the exhilaration and fervour with which it must have been uttered by the saintly bishop:

"Jesus, therefore, being wearied with his journey, sat there on the well. It was about the sixth hour." Now begin the mysteries. For it is not without a purpose that Jesus is weary; not indeed without a purpose that the strength of God is weary; not without a purpose that he is weary, by whom the wearied are refreshed; not without a purpose is he weary, by whose absence we are wearied, by whose presence we are strengthened. . . . It was for thee that Jesus was wearied with his journey. We find Jesus to be strength, and we find Jesus to be weak: we find a strong and a weak Jesus: strong because "in the beginning was the Word, and the Word was with God, and the Word was God: the same was in the beginning with God". Wouldst thou see how this Son of God is strong? "All things were made by him, and without him was nothing made": and without labour too, they were made. Then what can be stronger than he, by whom all things were made without labour? Wouldst thou know him weak? "The Word was made flesh, and dwelt among us." The strength of Christ created thee, the weakness of Christ created thee anew. The strength of Christ caused that to be which was not: the weakness of Christ caused that what was should not perish. He fashioned us by his strength, he sought us by his weakness.[9]

One further point remains to be considered, and it is one about which modern, as well as ancient thinkers have often felt at a loss to give a satisfactory answer. It concerns the physical appearance of Christ. The question is put as to whether Christ was of a striking and handsome, or, on the contrary, of a plain and even repellent appearance. A number of writers seem to attempt to answer this question according to their own ideas of what seems to them most fitting. One

[9] St Augustine, *Homily XV on St John's Gospel*, sect. 6 (trans. by Marcus Dods).

well-known contemporary writer, François Mauriac, is quite decided in his view:

> Concerning the physical appearance of Jesus, the Gospel account of the Passion gives us indirectly some information, for the tribune who came out in the night with the crowd from the High Priest, and with some soldiers of the cohort carrying torches, saw by the light of flames only a dark group of Jews and there was no one person who stood out, or appeared in any way remarkable. The Author of Life was just an ordinary bearded Nazarene, indistinguishable from the others, so that Judas had to point him out. For this purpose the man of Kerioth conceived the idea of embracing him: "He whom I shall kiss, that is He."[10]

One can easily detect in these finely written pages of Mauriac a striving after literary effect strained beyond measure for the sake of deciding a point of no apparent interest to the evangelists themselves. He sidesteps the real point of these events, and presents us with a highly imaginative account of the kiss of Judas in which he reconstructs the details to fit his own picture. At the opposite extreme to Mauriac's method of deciding the question is that of a few of the Fathers who take Psalm 44. 3 as providing a useful key: "Thine is more than mortal beauty, thy lips overflow with gracious utterance; the blessings God has granted thee can never fail." Their attempt to argue on the basis of this one text that Christ must have had the most splendid physical appearance is just wishful thinking.

The Gospels give us no direct information about Christ's physical appearance. They only tell us that during the Transfiguration the splendour of his divine nature permeated and marvellously enhanced his whole appearance, whatever that may have been. But why should we not take Christ's divine personality into consideration, and deduce as best we can the effects, even purely physical, that his human nature might reasonably be expected to have manifested just because it was the physical appearance of the nature hypostatically united to

[10] François Mauriac, *Vie de Jésus*, p. 248.

the Word of God himself? After all, was it not his majesty which made those of his fellow citizens of Nazareth, who wished to do away with him, stand away from him at a distance as if utterly powerless to touch the man who compelled profound respect even in those maliciously disposed towards him: "But he passed through the midst of them, and so went on his way" (Luke 4. 30)? Karl Adam tells us as much as we can glean from the Gospels themselves and what he says corroborates the conclusions we naturally draw:

> The powerful impression which Jesus made at sight on ordinary people and especially on the sick and on sinners certainly owed something to his attractive exterior, which by its charm drew everyone to him and held them, even if it was primarily due to his spiritual and religious power. His eyes with their burning, wakening, reproving looks must have been especially striking. Does not he himself say "the light of thy body is thy eye; if thy eye be single, thy whole body shall be lightsome" (Matt. 6. 22)? It is significant that Mark, when reporting some important saying of our Lord, not seldom uses some such expression as, "And looking round about on them he saith" (cf. Mark 3. 5; 34; 5. 32; 8. 33; 10. 21; 23. 27).[11]

We know that a face reflects quite involuntarily the soul which in some mysterious way is present within it. The splendour of a man's appearance is an exterior irradiation of an interior equilibrium, and physical graciousness is often a pure reflection of an interior excellence of soul. How can we refuse this physical splendour to the holiest of all the saints, "who knew no sin", and could experience no interior disorder? Such considerations certainly give us the more reason to venerate the physical humiliations freely suffered by our Lord during his passion, and to say with Fénelon: "You, the most wonderful of the sons of men, to what a sorry condition you have been reduced for the love of us!" By thinking of the physical horror of the wounds he suffered during his passion, and contrasting Christ crucified with the Christ who taught the multitudes, we

[11] Karl Adam, *The Son of God*, p. 90.

can understand something of St Paul's reproach of the senseless Galatians who had allowed themselves to become bewitched by false and deceitful charms: "who is it that has cast a spell on you, that you should refuse your loyalty to the truth, you, before whom Jesus Christ has been exposed to view on the cross?" (Gal. 3. 1).

THE HUMAN SOUL OF CHRIST

Of all the defects of human nature sin is without question the greatest. But paradoxically most men think that the power to sin, to be able to choose what is evil or what is good, is essential to one of our most noble and cherished possessions, namely our freedom. Hence we have straightway, without looking further afield, a number of problems concerning the perfection of Christ's human soul for which we must try to find a satisfactory solution. If Christ was incapable of sin, must he not have been without human freedom of will? Or, if he was free to choose for himself as we are, was he not capable, at least, of sinning even though in fact he never did sin?

First of all, the Scriptures state categorically that Christ was absolutely free not only from all sin, but also from the very possibility of sinning in any way. They allow for many weaknesses of our human nature being assumed by the Word, but always on the condition that they are not incompatible with the sanctity of God and the work of our redemption. Christ was like to us in all things "save only sin" (Heb. 4. 15; also 7. 26; 1 Peter 1. 19). There is no room for any doubt on this matter. Jesus himself was able to challenge the Pharisees with the question "which of you shall convince me of sin?" (John 8. 46) with complete assurance of the impossibility of their being able to make any charge against him. Among the modern critics Renan, in a well-known passage, the conclusion of which is plainly ambiguous, was not able to refrain from paying tribute to Christ's sanctity:

Mankind generally presents the picture of a crowd of people, low, egoistic, superior to the animals in this alone that their egoism is quite deliberate. However, from the midst of this universal vulgarity a few figures stand out like vast columns rising towards heaven and reminding man of some noble destiny before him. Jesus is the highest of them all in manifesting to men whence he came and whither he is going. In him is all that there is of good and all that is elevated in our nature.[12]

The Christian who reflects on his faith in the doctrine of the hypostatic union can see that the impeccability of Christ is absolutely inevitable because Christ is God, and God is absolutely incapable of sinning in any way. All the actions of Christ are the actions of the divine Person of the Word; they must therefore be superlatively holy. Furthermore, Christ willed to give us in himself a living example of every virtue he could require from us, and the very standards he set for us would necessarily exclude even the semblance of moral defect in the example he set us: "But you are to be perfect, as your heavenly Father is perfect" (Matt. 5. 48). He gave us the example of the perfect life the Father demands of us. The utter sinlessness of Christ's life on earth impresses on our minds the divinity of his sacred Person, and the absolute integrity of his human nature in which there was not even the slightest tendency towards sin.

But, someone may ask, what are we to make of the statement of St Paul in 2 Cor. (5. 21): "Christ never knew sin, and God made him into sin for us, so that in him we might be turned into the holiness of God"? As always, when we find an obscure text in Scripture which seems to conflict with solidly established truths of theology, we must study the obscure text in the light of others which are clear and mutually consistent. By following this general rule of exegesis our study of the obscure text will probably show that it contains shades of meaning we never at first suspected, particularly when we recognize that its obscurity may be due to a semitic way of thinking and speaking completely unlike our own. In 1 Cor. St Paul had written of Jesus Christ "whom God gave us to be

[12] E. Renan, *Vie de Jésus*, p. 77.

our wisdom, our justification, our sanctification and our atonement" (1. 30), so we can be quite certain that when he came
to write his second Epistle to the same Corinthian people he
would not openly contradict any important statement he had
made about Christ in the first Epistle. It seems that we have a
perfectly satisfactory explanation of this difficult text in the
interpretation which St Augustine gave of it, and which the
eleventh Council of Toledo accepted, that God made Christ
sin, not in the sense that he put sin into Christ (which would be
absurd), but in the sense that God made him the victim for the
sins of the world by willing that he should die on the cross to
atone for sin. Is it not said in Osee (4. 8) of the priests, who,
according to the law, ate the victims offered for sin: "it (sin)
was but the meat and drink such priests craved for"? St Paul
also wrote of God "sending us his own Son, in the fashion of
our own guilty nature, to make amends for our guilt" (Rom.
8. 3).[13] St Peter uses the same way of speaking of Christ as the
victim for our sins when he is writing about the sufferings of
Christ, emphasizing the stark realism of his humiliations. He
says: "it was thus that Christ died as a ransom, paid once for
all, on behalf of our sin, *he the innocent for us the guilty*, so
as to present us in God's sight. In his mortal nature he was
done to death, but endowed with fresh life in the spirit . . ."
(1 Peter 3. 18). Christ, then, was said by St Paul to be made
sin in as much as on the cross he presented all sinners in himself as their victim to his Father, and so made atonement in
himself to the Father of all mankind.

Though quite emphatic in their teaching about the impeccability of our Lord, the Gospels nonetheless relate the temptations he suffered from the devil at the beginning of his public
ministry. The synoptic Gospels describe them with a disarming
simplicity and complete sincerity which make any doubt about
their historical truth impossible (Matt. 4. 1–11; Mark 1. 12–13;
Luke 4. 1–13). The temptations were not isolated incidents

[13] St Augustine, *Enchiridion*, ch. 41. This is also the interpretation of
St Thomas, *Summa Theologica*, III, qu. 5, art. 1 ad 4. For the interpretation of the eleventh Council of Toledo, see Denziger, 286.

without any bearing on his future life, but trials experienced by Christ in connection with his mission as the promised Messiah and Redeemer. The evangelists always took pains to show how from the beginning of his public life Jesus refused to accept the rôle of a purely sensational miracle-working Messiah. Even at the very end of his sojourn on earth, immediately before his Ascension, Christ rejected the idea of making a spectacular self-manifestation by thrusting himself on people in such a way that they would have no option but to accept him. When the apostles, realizing the divine powers of Christ risen from the dead, asked him "dost thou mean to restore the dominion to Israel here and now?" he quietly set their query aside as idle (Acts 1. 6).

The temptations of our Lord in the desert show the devil attempting to lure him away at the very beginning of his ministry from his true redemptive mission by putting before him the advantages of appearing to the world as a non-suffering, spectacular miracle-working leader of his people. Now the theologian is presented with the question as to how these temptations of our Lord could be genuine, for if he was holy and impeccable as God himself it seems he could not possibly be lured into sin at all. One principle must guide our steps in seeking the solution to this problem. It is the absolute impossibility of any temptation arising for our Lord from a disorder within his human nature. Christ could never be lured towards, nor attracted by any evil whatever by anything happening within him. But there was nothing to prevent our Lord being subjected to a purely external temptation, that is to say, undergoing a trial of his bodily or mental integrity from some source wholly external to him. Thus the devil could present arguments of a certain apparent value which Christ could understand perfectly well, though they would not be able to stir any impulse within him to follow a specious argument his reason rejected. God could perfectly well have permitted temptations of this kind to assail him so that his sanctity could be made the more evident from the manner in which he drove the tempter and his assaults away. St Paul reminds us in Hebrews (4. 15) that it was appropriate that Christ the Saviour should have been tried in this way so that he could be the model to his disciples who, during all ages, would find strength in their own temptations from the memory of Christ's resistance to the suggestions of the evil one. But we must not imagine that because he could be tempted in some way, Christ could be tempted in the same kind of way as a sinful man. For men temptation arises from weakness; for Christ it was but an occasion for the manifestation of that inward strength he used in self-defence against his enemies when they tried to take advantage of a human infirmity he chose to suffer as an ordinary man.

The absence of all interior disorders within the soul of Christ, and the impossibility of any temptations arising from within himself are, of course, due to his being the Person of the Word and to the virginal conception by which he was born without original sin. How can we suppose that a man begotten by the power of the Holy Spirit could be affected in any way by original sin? The formation of his body and soul by the power of the Holy Spirit would of itself preserve him from any association with sin. Christ's entire human nature was at every moment of its existence under the sanctifying influence of the Holy Spirit; it was always the possession of the Word of God. The possibility of an interior concupiscence in Christ is only conceivable to one who is prepared to return to the Nestorian duality of natures and persons in Christ, the Person of the Word being sinless, and that of the man liable to sin. Nestorius did in fact hold that "Christ suffered the burden of the passions of the soul and desires of the flesh". Though the entire Catholic world has always regarded it with horror, the idea that Christ was liable to sin is often present in men's minds, and seems to haunt certain thinkers. On the very page on which we find the noble tribute to Christ's appearance, quoted earlier in this chapter, Renan also wrote: "Christ was not impeccable; *he conquered the passions we for ever fight*;

no angel comforted him, nor did he have any comfort save from his own conscience. No devil tempted him, save that which he, like each of us, bears in his own heart."[14] We might well ask ourselves with what spectacles Renan read the Gospels. But what is there to prevent anyone thinking in this kind of way, if, with his eyes wide open, he has denied that Christ is God?

In recent times some popular authors have written in much less restrained terms. Regarding sex as something perfectly natural, they have actually gone so far as to suggest that Christ must have experienced a man's natural desires of concupiscence just as he experienced hunger, thirst and fatigue. They accuse Catholics of being unrealistic in exalting continence, and refuse to reverence Christ for the virtue or practice of celibacy, of which Christians regard him as the model.

The Fathers had to face occasional questions of this kind and they deal with them quite adequately. It seems extraordinary that it should be necessary in these days of advanced psychological studies to point out the difference, between "disordered desire" and "attraction". A disordered sexual desire is not natural to man as such, but the effect of original sin, whereas the attraction of a person of one sex for persons of the opposite sex is perfectly natural and good—it is so normal and healthy that it is just a part of human life. It only becomes unhealthy with abnormal people who do not understand or observe the elementary rules of temperance and self-control. A mere attraction for people of the opposite sex is human; but it is not inhuman for a man to be free from sexual passions or to observe perfect continence. Linked as it is with the practice of moral virtues based on the cardinal virtue of temperance—abstinence, fasting, sobriety, kindness, industriousness—continence has never been regarded by healthy people as involving any extraordinary or inhuman strain. It may, in fact, become a necessity of daily life for anyone who suffers bereavement in marriage. It is lamentable having to

[14] E. Renan, *op. cit.*, p. 77.

recall these elementary truths, but they must be kept in mind by anyone who strives to appreciate the sinlessness of Christ's human nature.

Many modern thinkers regard the Christian virtue of chastity as a weakness revealing the Christian's fear of life. Those who do so confuse Christian with Manichean doctrine. Only one with a superficial knowledge of Catholic life and thought could find anything Manichean in the asceticism of the first centuries of the Christian Church. Voluntary continence has always been held in honour by the Church, not because of any rejection or disdain for human life which she treasures as a gift of God—this disdain may be a characteristic of certain forms of Greek philosophy, but it is alien to the Judaeo-Christian theology of the Bible—but when accepted as a means to a higher end and as a free consecration of the body to the glory of God. The first Christian ascetics vowed themselves to chastity in order, to quote the beautiful words of St Ignatius of Antioch, "to give honour to the flesh, which is the Lord's".[15] How could they consider giving such honour to Christ's flesh and human life if they disdain human life and flesh, or if they regard Christ's flesh as affected by the least disorder? So few non-Christians ever realize that for a Christian morality is not just a matter of being obedient to a law which is external to and imposed on man, but first and foremost a way of living "in Christ Jesus", in the way described by St Paul.

We know from the Gospels that Christ did not treat with disdain the human attraction which exists between people of opposite sexes, for it is an integral part of our human nature which needs nothing carnal to express the friendships to which it may give rise. Did he disdain the presence of his Mother with whom he lived for about thirty years of his short life? Did he decline the attentive care of the holy women who followed him during his Galilean ministry? Did he scorn the ministrations of Mary Magdalen as she anointed his feet and

[15] St Ignatius, *Letter to Polycarp*, sect. 5.

wiped them with her tears? Did he not rejoice in the company of Martha and Mary as well as Lazarus their brother? The least assiduous readers of the Gospels should know enough of Christ to realize that he is absolutely innocent of the "churlish misogynism" which is sometimes characteristic of ascetics. His meetings with womenfolk were characterized by a simplicity and spontaneous directness which reveal the perfect self-mastery and the uprightness of his human nature. Christ loved women as he loved men. Experience of the lives of the saints amply confirms the reality of such self-mastery among mere men whose lives were perfectly ruled by divine grace. One example will illustrate the truth of this: the supernatural friendship of St John of the Cross for his spiritual daughters, Doña del Mercada at Segovia and the Carmelite Nuns at Beas. To the first he dedicated his "Living Flame of Love"; a question put to him in the parlour of the Carmel of Beas by a girl of twenty was the occasion of his writing the last five strophes of his "Spiritual Canticle". If the meeting of "the royal souls"[16] was able to call forth such strains and marvels of poetic utterance in the expression of their love of God and of the graces of mystical union in a disciple of Christ, can we not say that their friendship was based on a perfection of soul which was just a reflection of the far more wondrous equilibrium in the attraction experienced by Christ in his human soul for the women, like Martha and Mary, with whom he was on terms of close friendship? Is not the attraction of the disciple, and the most exemplary of disciples, based on that of the Master?

St Basil expressed the mind of all the Fathers of the Church on this matter admirably:

> It is evident that the Lord accepted and assumed the natural passions of a man to confirm our faith in the genuineness of the Incarnation, and to show that it was not purely imaginary. But the passions which exist in man as the result of sin and which affect the integrity of our lives, Christ repudiated as unworthy

[16] The expression belongs to Fr Lucian of Mary and Joseph, in his edition of the *Complete Works of St John of the Cross* (Édition Bibliothèque Européenne, p. 649).

of his spotless divinity. This explains why the Apostle (Paul) wrote that "Christ was born *in the likeness* of sinful flesh and not in sinful flesh".[17]

CHRIST'S HUMAN FREEDOM AND TWO WILLS

Some of the most mysterious of all the prerogatives of Christ's human nature are connected with his human will. His human will is certainly different from his divine will, and the difference is not merely one of fact, but an intrinsic necessity. Will is an endowment of an intelligent nature; as Christ has two different natures he must have two different wills, a divine and a human will, but by reason of the hypostatic union both wills belong to the Person of the Word Incarnate. In the Blessed Trinity there is but one will common to the Three Persons as these Persons are one nature; but in Christ there are two different natures, and thus two different wills.

The Gospels reveal beyond any question the presence of two wills in Christ. To witness our Lord's use of both his wills we have only to recall the Gospel account of our Lord's agony in the Garden of Gethsemani, recorded by all three synoptic Gospels but most vividly by St Luke. He tells us of many important incidents during the Agony such as his sweat of blood and the coming of the angel to comfort our Lord, not mentioned by the other evangelists, but the narrative of all three evangelists is centred on the conflict which went on within Christ and which can only be understood as a conflict of wills. Christ speaks of his human will and of his human desire that the chalice may pass him by. Thus in his human nature he recoils before the imminent threat of his passion; but he contrasts this human will with the will by which he accepts whatever the Father willed: "My Father, if it is possible, let this chalice pass me by; only as thy will is, not as mine" (Matt. 26. 39; Luke 22. 42). Earlier in his life Christ had spoken

---

[17] St Basil, *Epistle* 261 (*P.G.* 32, col. 972). See St Thomas Aquinas, *Contra Gentes*, Book 4, ch. 29, on St Paul's words "the likeness of sinful flesh".

in the same way: "It is the will of him who sent me, not my own will, that I have come down from heaven to do" (John 6. 38). The Father's will is, of course, one and the same as his own divine will, so the struggle was clearly one between his own two wills. Our Lord accepted the will of the Father, but at the moment when the commandments of the Father actually laid the severe burdens of self-sacrifice on him, he experienced with his human will a desire to follow an easier path. This conflict of wills in Christ, however, was not a radical discord or opposition of wills by which each was set upon opposed objectives.

Christ did not reject with his human will what the divine will was intent on doing or reaching. On the contrary Christ chose with his human will what he chose with his divine will (which, it must be remembered, was identical with the will of the Father): the conflict was due to an inevitable difficulty which Christ's lower or purely human will, since it was intimately associated with the natural tendencies of his sensitive human nature, had in adapting itself to his higher divine Will, which was irrevocably set on accepting all the sufferings which Christ knew he had to bear in offering himself in sacrifice on the cross. If Christ had not experienced this difficulty he would not have been human at all, he would not, indeed, have had a human will at all. Christ's whole human nature recoiled quite naturally at the prospect of the death which lay before him, making the full and free acceptance, by his human will, of imminent death by crucifixion, supremely difficult. The agony he experienced in the Garden consisted in the effort to maintain in his human will the firmness of its very adherence to the divine will, by restraining the natural dread of his purely sensitive nature at the prospect of the physical torments which lay before him. Here is St Matthew's account of Christ's terrible agony:

> So Jesus came, and they with him, to a plot of land called Gethsemani; and he said to his disciples, sit down here, while I go in there and pray. But he took Peter and the sons of Zebedee

with him. And now he grew sorrowful and dismayed; My soul, he said, is ready to die with sorrow, do you abide here, and watch with me. When he had gone a little further, he fell upon his face in prayer, and said, My Father, if it is possible, let this chalice pass me by; only as thy will is, not as mine. Then he went back to his disciples, to find them asleep; and he said to Peter, Had you no strength, then, to watch with me even for an hour? Watch and pray, that you may not enter into temptation; the spirit is willing enough, but the flesh is weak. Then he went back again, and prayed a second time; and his prayer was, My Father, if this chalice may not pass me by, but I must drink it, then thy will be done. And once more he found his disciples asleep when he came to them, so heavy their eyelids were; this time he went away without disturbing them, and made his third prayer, using the same words. After that he returned to his disciples, and said to them, Sleep and take your rest hereafter; as I speak, the time draws near when the Son of Man is to be betrayed into the hands of sinners. Rise up, let us go on our way; already, he that is to betray me is close at hand (Matt. 26. 34–46).

Christian piety of every age has reflected deeply and with profound reverence on the anguish of Jesus in the Garden. Cardinal Newman wrote one of his most remarkable sermons on the mental sufferings of our Lord in his passion, which must have been the fruit of years of prayerful contemplation of this awesome mystery.[18] Pascal saw in our Lord's agony "the torments which he inflicted on himself", and he saw in Christ's own agony the sufferings of his mystical Body, for "Jesus will be in agony till the end of the world".[19] Ambricourt, dear to the heart of Bernanos, the story of whose inner life he wrote, felt himself "at the place chosen from all eternity, and the prisoner of the Holy Agony". . . .[20] But if Christian piety is strengthened by the example of our Lord, and by the way he sympathized with our human wretchedness to the point of

[18] See J. H. Newman, *Discourses to Mixed Congregations.*
[19] Pascal, *Pensées,* 553.
[20] G. Bernanos, *Diary of a Country Priest,* ch. 6. The Agony of Christ is a favourite theme of this famous novelist.

experiencing its extreme of mental and physical pain, it is nonetheless the privilege of the most devout to seek some understanding of the mystery which it reverences very deeply.

First of all, we must show, as the Third Council of Constantinople taught,[21] that the distinction of wills in Christ cannot involve any opposition of one to the other. Christ's human will was always in perfect accord with the divine will. As he said so often, "I have come from heaven not to do my own will, but the will of him who sent me", and in the Garden Christ followed with his human will the will of the Father saying that as man he chose "as thy will is, not as mine is". The conformity of the two wills follows simply from the fact that both wills belong to one and the same divine Person of the Word who wills with his human will what he wills as God. A theory of opposition of two wills in Christ would contradict the teaching of Scripture, and it would logically lead to Nestorianism, for as choice is an act of a person, conflicting choices would inevitably involve a duality of persons at variance with each other. But the necessity for preserving the conformity of the human to the divine will in Christ must not be pushed to the opposite extreme of Monophysitism, either by saying that the two wills were so harmonized as to be really commingled to the point of being really but one will (this is Monothelitism), or by thinking of the human will as being purely passive under the control of the divine will.[22]

The moral union of the two wills does not destroy their metaphysical diversity, even if they act together because both belong to the one Person of the Word. The Third Council of Constantinople defined:

> We must acknowledge in Christ two wills and activities belonging to two natures, undivided, mutually unchangeable, inseparable and distinct. Such is the doctrine of the Holy Fathers. The human will follows the divine and all-powerful will without opposition or resistance, and with submission. In

[21] Denzinger, 289–93.
[22] See Karl Adam, *The Christ of Faith*, pp. 40–3; 211–13.

fact, as the wise Athanasius said, it was necessary that Christ's human will should move itself, but in submitting to the divine will. For just as his flesh is called the flesh of the Word of God and is so truly, so the Word himself said "I have come from heaven not to do my own will, but the will of him who sent me, the Father". He thus calls his own the will which is proper to his human nature, for the human nature to which the human will belongs he has taken to himself. Just as, in fact, the spotless and holy human nature of Christ is not destroyed by being deified, but rather maintained in its proper nature and state, so his human will is preserved intact, though it is deified because it belongs to God. St Gregory Nazianzen wrote accurately that "the human will of the Saviour is not contrary to God, but it is wholly divinized".[23]

The agony of our Lord certainly shows the genuine distinction of the two wills; it does not show that they were set in opposition to each other by contradictory choices. A reflection on our own experience in face of difficulties may help us here to attain some understanding of what our Lord experienced in his agony. We all know of the way in which our reason or conscience can find itself at odds with our sensible nature; the weakness of our nature inclines us to follow the alluring attractions of sense rather than the more difficult judgements of right and wrong which our conscience would have us respect. The human nature of Christ, confirmed in good by grace, could not experience a conflict of this kind between right and wrong, for there was no disorder within Christ by which his human, sensitive nature could seek something evil or even follow an inclination over which his mind and will might lose control. His human nature was the immaculately pure nature of the Word of God free from all disordered inclinations. But in his human nature Christ could feel the natural, spontaneous and involuntary movements of human sensitivity, especially those recoiling from evil, even mere physical evils. These movements of revulsion would be analogous to those which we experience when, confronted with the necessity of undergoing a very

[23] See Denzinger, 291.

painful operation, we are brought face to face with the actual ordeal as it is about to commence. Nonetheless our higher rational will can impose its decisions on the lower inclinations, with their sensations and lively feelings, and we can make them submit to what they naturally abhor. Now, we can ask ourselves, what kind of struggle or inward torment did Jesus experience in the Garden as he was about to face the ordeal of his passion? So long as "his hour" had not come close upon him, he could avoid the apprehension of the horrors of his death by not thinking too much about it. But on the evening of Maundy Thursday he was as a man who knew that he was being "enclosed in a hopeless trap, which the Garden of Gethsemani had suddenly become for him. He was condemned to die by the will of his Father, oppressed by evil spirits of Satan, sacrificed to death by his own act of self-sacrifice, his whereabouts were known to Judas, and the garden was being completely encircled by the armed force sent from the Jewish Temple."[24] How could Christ's human nature possibly not feel anguish at the prospect of imminent torments, especially as his human mind with its supreme clarity of vision enabled him to know how desperate, from the human point of view, his position had become? The involuntary sensations of a man caught in a trap by enemies intent on his life permeate the whole of his being and betray themselves in every action he performs. It is true that Christ willed to fall into the trap set by his enemies, but God's will did not permit Christ's human experience of the trap to be fictitious; on the contrary, it was by his own will that he experienced it as a real trap. Thus Jesus declared at the height of his torment: "My soul is sad unto death." But all through the agony Christ held his sensitive human nature under the complete control of his reason, so that no matter how intense the conflict, it never became a conflict with a disordered nature. His human will accepted at each moment with perfect control what his sensitive nature abhorred.

[24] P. Lavergne, *Synopse Française*, p. 229.

Thus the union of the two wills in Christ is not the meta-physical fusion of two powers into one, but the acceptance by two distinct powers of one and the same end. It is impossible to conclude that the two wills are really only one from the fact that both pursue the same objective. "When I say that my will and somebody else's will are one, I mean to say that we strive after the same object, that we love the same object, that we agree about the same object; so in Christ there never was, and there never could be, two wills in the sense of two conflicting and contradictory objects: whatever was willed by Divinity was also willed by Humanity. Such an identification of wills is a perfection; but, on the contrary, fusion of wills as powers would be a great loss; in fact it would be the destruction of nature."[25] With his human will our Lord accepted the necessity of the redemption which was before his mind: during his public life he had spoken now and then of the time of his sacrifice as "his hour", as the essential thing in his whole lifework, and as the reason for which he had become a man at all. His wills could not possibly be at cross-purposes with regard to this supreme objective, for, as the Scriptures affirm many times, it was on this that Christ was set with the whole of his being, human and divine (John 12. 27–28; 10. 15).

To explain yet further how the two distinct wills in Christ act together in one moral unity of purpose, St Thomas has recourse to an idea that was very familiar during the Middle Ages, and which he applied to his whole theology of our Lord's human nature: this is the idea of an instrumental cause. An instrument, in the proper sense of the term, may seem to many people nowadays to be something purely mechanical which works on its own once a few levers have been pulled. The word conjures up something in the nature of an adding machine or an automatic reckoner. For the medieval theologians, how-ever, and generally for mankind at large, an instrument is a thing which a man uses for doing some work, which he appropriates to himself by linking it with his own hands and

[25] A. Vonier, *op. cit.*, ch. xiv (i, p. 142).

brain so that he may manipulate it personally in the actual work of producing some effect. For example, an artist's hands are the instruments he uses to bring into being the work he conceives in his mind. The hands of Michelangelo or of Paderewski wrought the marvels they conceived in their minds, and that lived inwardly in their imaginations. Their works came from their minds and their hands, or from their hands as directed by their minds.

An artist's hands are instruments intrinsic to him, but to produce his works he needs the use of other instruments extrinsic to him, such as a piano or chisel. In the actual execution of his work these instruments become almost a part of him, as though they were a kind of addition to his hands extending their latent powers. The artist uses hand and chisel as one complex instrument he has at the service of his mind and imagination. The artist's mind works in his hands and through his chisel on his materials. These familiar examples of instrumental causality can be remarkably helpful, if carefully used, in bringing us to see the rôle of Christ's human nature, and particularly of his human will, in his work of accomplishing our redemption. A human nature, and thus a human will, were assumed by the Word as "instruments he conjoined to his divinity", as instruments, which in virtue of the hypostatic union, were inseparably united to the Person of the Son of God for his work of redeeming us, even as the hands of the pianist are the instruments intrinsic to him which he uses to play his music. As an artist's hands work in union with his brain and are directed by him, so Christ used his human will to choose as man all that he willed as God. Without his human nature the Word could not have suffered nor redeemed us, any more than without his hands an artist could produce music for others to hear. By means of his body and entire human nature the Word was able to bring about the redemption. He suffered, died and rose again *as man*. The cross and the other instruments of the passion were like extrinsic instruments he made use of as he accomplished the work of our salvation, even as the piano or chisel are the instruments the artist makes his own for the purpose of his work.

The conception of Christ's human nature, which is of capital importance in the Christology of St Thomas, provides us with the secret of the close union of the two wills in Christ, showing that though they differed in their natures, they were united in their activities. With his human will Christ willed just what as the Word he willed with his divine will, since he only assumed a human will that he might accomplish through it, as with a subordinate instrument, what he willed to accomplish with his divine will. We find this union of wills in all the works which Christ brought about through the powers of his two natures, for example, his miracles, his teaching, his offering of his life for our salvation.

"And now a leper came and knelt before him, and said, Lord, if it be thy will, thou hast power to make me clean. Jesus held out his hand and touched him, and said, It is my will; be thou made clean. Whereupon the leprosy was immediately cleansed" (Matt. 8. 2–4; Mark 1, 40–43; Luke, 5. 12–13).

St Thomas explains the nature of the instrumental rôle of Christ's human nature at length in the *Summa Theologica*. He writes, for example:

> The action of an instrument as such is one with that of the principal agent for it just enables the principal agent to produce the work for which he uses the instrument. So therefore the activities of Christ's human nature precisely as instrumental, and therefore as directed by the Word through his divine nature, are one with the activities of his divine nature: for the salvation by which the human nature of Christ saves is not different from that by which his divine nature saves.[26]

This teaching of St Thomas about Christ's human will and its instrumental rôle in his activities will probably surprise many people who, thinking that freedom must involve the power to choose between good and evil as contraries, will see that Christ's human freedom could not possibly have been free

[26] St Thomas, *Summa Theologica*, III, qu. 19, art. 1, ad 2.

to choose evil because he used his human will purely instru-
mentally as a kind of prolongation of his divine will. Furthermore, they may ask themselves, apart altogether from the fact
that Christ was impeccable while on earth—and it is certain
that he was—how could he have been free, since as man he
could not choose anything but what he knew the Father had
willed him to choose as man? If he could only choose the
good, and it is surely necessary to hold that, he must surely
have had the power to choose as man the means by which he
would bring about the end the Father imposed on him, so that,
for example, he could accomplish the work of our redemption
by some means of his own choice.

To meet these difficulties the theologian distinguishes two
things:

(a) The way in which a choice is made, and

(b) The way in which the divine action influences created
beings, and the created human will.

(a) It is undeniable that freedom lies in the power to make a
choice, and that for us men the choice lies very often between
ends which are contradictorily opposed as good and evil. But
the power to choose between such contradictories does not
belong to freedom as such. It is due rather to some special
defect in our human freedom, for evil as such is not an object
which merits choice even when it is treated as a good of some
kind. It is more perfect to choose between good things without
being able to choose evil, than to be able to choose between
evil as well as good things, for the power to choose good is a
perfection, but power to choose an evil is an imperfection. To
be able to choose good *and* evil is not a greater perfection than
to be able to choose solely between goods, for evil is not a
perfection. The choosing of good and evil is really the choosing
of good or the rejecting of good: and the word "and" in the
expression "good and evil" is deceptive, for it is not an addition, but a subtraction. It is more perfect to live without being
able to suffer sickness or death, than to live and be liable to
sickness or death. No one in his senses would prefer the latter
to the former.

The good determines the will to act: the essential prerogative of freedom, then, lies in the power to choose the good which befits an intellectual being. If a man does not choose the good which befits his nature in its wholeness and fullness, he chooses some particular good which attracts him, but in doing so he must blind himself to the good of his nature in its wholeness and fullness. If he allows himself to be so blinded, he may succeed in persuading himself that some particular good which entices him is really for the good of his whole self and being. By seeking a particular good as though it was his whole good, and placing his whole good in some particular thing which really excludes what is for his whole good, a man is able to make a choice which is really the choice of what is evil for him. This difference between a person's whole good and some particular good is easily grasped. On a hot summer's day my present, immediate and particular good may lie in drinking some kind of iced beverage to quench a powerful thirst and indulge a favourite kind of taste. While I feel the thirst I may know that, as a result of taking this particular drink, I will almost certainly suffer from acute digestive trouble for several days, for, alas, this most desirable of drinks does not suit me. But I may allow the attraction of this special drink to attract me so powerfully that I put from my mind all thought of the possible sufferings it will bring me later in the week. This drink really does not agree with me at all, but I may choose to take it with my eyes on nothing but the present enjoyment it will bring to me. Now, who is going to say that, though I am free to take it if I will, I am making good use of my freedom in deciding to take it rather than another kind of drink? Would I not be much better off as a man if I freely chose a drink which suits me, and if I had disciplined my tastes so that they would not incline me to make choices which ill suit me? It might in certain cases even be preferable not to have such freedom if its persistent misuse is going to involve me in very serious and perhaps irreparable losses.

This disorder in our wills which puts the abuse of freedom

within our power is not irreparable, provided we consider seriously in all that we do the good of our whole being or whole self, choosing particular things as means leading us to our supreme end, and ordering our lives freely by the choices we make between goods which are genuine values to us. Now we have already seen at what exalted heights the human nature of Christ lived by reason of its hypostatic union with the Word: the whole of Christ's moral life as a man was set within the scheme of God's purpose for redeeming man from sin. Christ's human mind saw and understood so clearly the absolute and universal good which was presented to it in the Father's will that he should redeem us by his death on the cross.

The Father's will was presented to his human mind as the supreme good for him as man, and for acceptance as such by his human will. His will was so free from any disorder of any kind that it was just inevitable that he should choose as man what he had chosen as God, and in so choosing he exercised his freedom in a way that was superior to that in which we exercise ours, because for him the possibility of misusing his freedom by rejecting his Father's will did not even exist. But what Christ chose as man he chose with full human knowledge and complete satisfaction *by an act of which he had full mastery,* and therein lay its real freedom. Thus our Lord said: "This my Father loves in me, that I am laying down my life, to take it up again afterwards. Nobody can rob me of it; I lay it down of my own accord. I am free to lay it down, free to take it up again; that is the charge which my Father has given me" (John 10. 17–18).

Because of the hypostatic union Christ's human mind enjoyed the unceasing vision of God himself: as a consequence he could not suffer any mental blindness preventing him from seeing the absolute good of the Father's will, nor could his mind become entranced by the spectacle of a particular, relative or created good. Hence, there was no possibility of any other good usurping the place of the supreme good in his mind. The experienced mountaineer who knows with absolute certainty the way to the mountain summit picks out his route without worrying either about the sharp bends which hide his ultimate objective temporarily from view, or the illusory minor summits which may lead a novice to mistake them for the real summit. He seeks the real summit freely and inevitably without erring. For Christ, our way and our guide, the "interior master" of his human will was the Word of God, and therein lay the secret both of his impeccability and his freedom.

(b) The supreme theological principle St Thomas always uses when considering the influence of the divine action on created human wills is that "God always moves free creatures that they may act freely, for God moves each being according to its nature". This, of course, is the cardinal principle of the theory of physical premotion, by which the Thomists claim they preserve the balance between God's sovereign Lordship as the ultimate source of all good, and man's freedom in doing morally good actions. If a man's free choice is good, then in some way God causes that good action, though it belongs also to the man who does the action. The essential point is that God's influence on the will enables the man to perform his act in its very freedom. The mystery lies wholly in the reality of the divine "influence" which surpasses our understanding, just as much as the divine Being with which it is, of course, identical. To be able to understand clearly and in detail how God moves our will to its good actions, but in such a way that our complete freedom of action is guaranteed, and at the same time that the choice made is our own, we would have to know God's creative act as it is. St Thomas expressed his idea in a statement which is not really the paradox it appears to be: No amount of divine *influxus* will ever do away with the ownership I have of my own actions: this *influxus* is of such a nature as to render my acts the more perfectly mine, though God enables me to do them. As we said, God moves each being in accordance with the nature he has given it; he moves a material being to act according to the necessities inherent in its nature,

and he moves a spiritual or free being to act freely according
to the requirements of its free nature.

A comparison made by Abbot Vonier may be usefully
quoted here: "Engineering skill has replaced the original banks
of many a stream with artificial embankments. There is no end
to the resources of the engineer; if he be given time and money,
he might replace the banks of the Rhine with stone dykes all
the way from Switzerland down to the North Sea. But no
engineer, even with an empire to finance him, would ever
replace the stream itself by one of his own invention."[27] If the
Gospels justify the principle of using parables and examples
in teaching men the supernatural truths of their faith, can we
not welcome this example to help us think as best we can of
the way in which Christ's human will was, in some mysterious
way, guided by the Personality of the Word to do just what
God willed, but to do it in a way that was free because God
moved his own human nature to act freely, and choose freely
what he divinely willed?

Theologians, even the Thomists themselves, give different
explanations of the way in which Christ exercised his free will.
Some have thought on the lines that we can conceive free acts
in Christ based on his infused or his acquired knowledge.
Others have preferred to stress the fact that Christ's mind
always enjoyed the beatific vision but that this did not deprive
him of his freedom with regard to created realities even though
they were seen in the divine essence. He spontaneously willed
and loved God and all that which in God is one with God's
essence. But created things whether they have been, are or will
be, were only secondary subjects for Christ to choose, and he
chose them as he saw them in God. God, who loves his own
perfect Being necessarily, is free to will or not to will these
created realities and his love for them is a love of choice. Thus,
Christ, in the beatific vision, could also freely love the created
objects that God loves and wills. Thus St Thomas wrote that
"the will of Christ, though determined to what is good, was

[27] A. Vonier, *op. cit.*, ch. vii (I, pp. 119–20).

not determined to this or that particular good; Christ could choose by his free will confirmed in the good this or that object as he willed, just like the blessed in heaven".[28]

In conclusion, we can say with Fr Héris, O.P., "fixed once and for all in God, this human will of Christ could will nothing other than God willed and as God willed it: what God necessarily willed, it necessarily willed; what God freely willed, it freely willed. Thus it remained like God's will with regard to the created objects which were the object of his love, permeated with a sovereign indifference towards the thing considered in itself and apart from God, so that he chose them solely for God's sake without ever departing from what had been willed by the eternal ordinance of God. Thus we see the perfect love of Christ as man for his Father which made him seek and accomplish in all things his divine will: 'my food is to do the will of Him who sent me'."[29]

[28] St Thomas Aquinas, *Summa Theologica*, III, qu. 18, art. 4, ad 3.
[29] C. V. Héris, O.P., Notes in Volume III, p. 299 of *Le Verbe Incarné*, from the edition of the *Summa Theologica* published by the *Revue des Jeunes*.

CHAPTER VI

THE DIVINE AND HUMAN ACTIVITIES OF THE WORD INCARNATE

THE ACTIVITIES AND WORKS OF CHRIST

What reader of the Gospels can fail to notice, whatever else he may fail to note for want of due care in reading, the persistence with which Jesus claimed that his *works and deeds* are most evident signs and proofs of his divinity? The deeds and actions of Christ have the mark of God's own omnipotence upon them, and bear witness to the intimacy of his union with the Father who sent him: "If you find that I do not act like the son of my Father, then put no trust in me; but if I do, then let my actions convince you where I cannot; so you will recognize and learn to believe that the Father is in me, and I in him" (John 10. 37–8).

All the miracles of Christ are connected in some way with the supreme end of his life's mission on earth, that of redeeming men from sin. Yet more, every act in Christ's life bears the imprint of his Father's will upon it, and bears witness to Christ's human consciousness of the work of having to redeem man entrusted to him by the Father: "And he who sent me is with me; he has not left me all alone, since what I do is always what pleases him" (John 8. 29). Christ's activities made the presence of the Emmanuel, or God among men, perceptible to all. Thus our Lord often said that those who refuse to acknowledge this plain evidence of his works to his divinity did so from their own blind obstinacy. The only people who could fail to know him for what he claimed to be were the blind and those led by the blind. Christ would have us all ponder earnestly on the facts of God the Son in his human nature in which we can actually see God at work.

We have seen that in the God-man Jesus Christ there are two natures and, because each nature is complete, Christ possessed two wills in perfect accord with each other. We have now to explain that there were in Christ two different kinds of activity. The marvellous riches of the psychology of Christ are by no means exhausted when we have explained the theological principles governing his activities, but they are among the greatest of these riches. The psychology of Christ is indeed a subject for prayerful meditation as well as serious theological reflection. The Church's liturgical prayers are laden with thoughts about these treasures of faith. It is a matter for regret that vast numbers of Catholic people seem to be without any realization of the spiritual riches of these great prayers. Those who do use them know well enough that the theology of Christ's activities is not just a superfluous luxury or a piece of abstract speculation. Some knowledge of the activities of our Lord is necessary to all Catholics for a purely practical reason, in that without it we can scarcely have a proper appreciation of the efficacy of the sacraments in the sanctification of our own lives. The efficacy of the sacraments is due directly and immediately to the action of Christ. Let no one imagine, then, that in thinking about Christ's actions and works we are just turning aside to a topic of minor importance.[1]

During the controversies with Eutyches prior to the Council of Chalcedon, St Leo the Great, in his *Tome* to Flavian, laid down the principles governing the theology of Christ's actions. The full theological study of these principles, however, belongs

[1] See M. J. Nicolas, O.P., *What is the Eucharist?* pp. 38–9, in this series.

to the later period of medieval scholastic theology, and once again we shall turn to St Thomas for guidance in this as in all matters of Christology. St Leo determined: "Each 'form' (or nature) does the acts which belong to it, in communion with the other; the Word, that is, performing what belongs to the Word, and the flesh carrying out what belongs to the flesh; the one of these shines out in miracles, the other succumbs to injuries."[2]

The Third Council of Constantinople (held in 680), which condemned Monothelitism (or the doctrines that Christ had but one will, as the Monophysites had taught that he had but one nature), expressed the same principle yet more precisely: "The difference of the natures in the unique hypostasis of the Word is evident from the fact that each of them, in union with the other, wills and works its own effect. For this reason we confess two wills and two activities working together in Christ, just as befits the salvation of man."[3]

These words contain a wealth of theology which is surprising considering they are so few. They speak of the unity of Person in Christ, and the duality of his natures. Each nature is firmly stated to be real, and known to be real from the reality of its will made evident to all from the works it effects. The Council was obviously on its guard against the chances of Nestorianism or Monophysitism infiltrating once more into men's minds when they considered the problems of Christ's activities. The position at stake in rejecting Monothelitism, in which Sergius, the Patriarch of Constantinople, had become involved in the early part of the seventh century, was of capital importance especially when it is seen in the context of the purpose of the Incarnation in the plan of the Father, the salvation of mankind. If Christ's acts are not divine and human we are still left the sinners we were before the Incarnation. It is the oneness of the Person of Christ which made it possible for him to act both in a human nature with a human will and in his divine

[2] St Leo, *Tome*, ch. 4 (trans. by Canon William Bright).
[3] Denzinger. 292.

nature with his divine will. Christ's human nature, being united hypostatically to the Person of the Word, shared in, and even played a part in his divine acts and their effects. Christ, acting as God on earth, used his human nature and his human will in the accomplishment of his divine mission; with the aid of his human nature, and dependently on it, he performed his miracles, and brought about the sanctification and redemption of mankind. Our final glorification in heaven will also be the work of Christ, working thus as the God-man. In its definitions concerning the divine-human activity of Christ the Council of Constantinople put before us the nature of what is called the *theandric activity* of our Lord, and it laid the foundations on which St Thomas later constructed his theology of the instrumental causality of Christ's human nature in effecting our redemption.

St Thomas uses his idea of instrumental causality in dealing with many topics other than those connected with the psychology of Christ. As we have already said, the idea is of fundamental importance in the whole of his Christology, his theology of the sacraments and his doctrine concerning the divine economy of the redemption. The reader must, therefore, pardon our taking the topic up once more in even further detail, for we need it to reach an understanding of the mystery of the saving action of God on the souls of men.

We have seen already that an instrument which an artist uses only produces an artistic effect if it is closely united to, and brought under the control of the artist, or, in St Thomas' terminology, of the principal agent, so that in his hands it becomes as one with the artist himself. Now the control of the instrument by the artist does not deprive the instrument of its own specific activity, nor of its contribution to the effect produced by the artist. On the contrary, the artist makes use of, and gets the best out of the instrument and what it can be made to do, so that the effect comes simultaneously both from the artist as the principal, and the instrument as a secondary cause. Thus the music comes both from the pianist and the piano;

the better the piano the better the tonal qualities of the music the pianist plays on it. An instrument serves the principal agent by reason of the qualities it has, and instruments, so far from being just interchangeable *ad libitum*, are selected according to the excellence of what they can do. One can only expect of each instrument what it is capable of producing, and any artist who has a good instrument treasures it in preference to most others. The instrument itself, however, is dead so long as the artist is not actually using it: it is just a thing that will act when someone uses it. Of itself it produces nothing. From the moment an artist does use it, however, it acquires an effectiveness beyond its own inherent capacities, in that it becomes, as it were, a part of the artist himself as he infuses his own active powers into it; the artist acts on and through his instrument, directing precisely how every movement in each of its parts is to be made, just as though he had become incarnate in it himself, and in so acting he produces his works. As thus united to the artist the instrument can be made to produce effects proportioned to the powers of the artist, heightened and enhanced as they are by his making the instrument as much a part of himself as he can.

The pianist at play and his piano form one complex unit of activity: so that the music comes as much from the piano as from the pianist. The music is made as such by the pianist, but the music he makes comes from the piano, and is conditioned by the qualities of the piano. The effect produced, the music the audience listens to, is "specified" by the kind of instrument the musician uses and the qualities of sound it produces under the artist's fingers. The same music played by the same artist on a piano, an harmonium and a large pipe organ sounds different. In other words, the action of the instrument may be strictly subordinate to, and under the control of, that of the principal agent, but the nature of the instrument he is using conditions the action of the agent, and contributes qualities of its own to the effect he produces. Thus the principal agent can claim that the effect he produces by means of the instrument he uses is his own, but he must acknowledge his indebtedness to his instrument which contributes to his effect qualities which are plainly recognizable in the effect. Thus St Thomas says that it is the chisel used by the sculptor that cuts the marble and so enables the sculptor to produce a statue; but there is a close fusion of the two actions (principal and instrumental) into *one* complex action producing the total effect which is the work of art.[4]

With this example in mind we can now turn once more to the activities of our Lord Jesus Christ. The activity of Christ is of capital interest in Christology, for in our reflections on his activities we are able to see, in a particular concrete form, the explicative value of the dogmatic principles of the mystery of the hypostatic union studied in chapter III. In other words, so far from leaving behind, we are still considering the union of two natures in the one Person of the Word, but from a dynamic point of view. Clearly, then, anyone who begins to think of Christ's activities with false ideas of nature or person in Christ, will be thinking on lines similar to those of Nestorius or Eutyches. We trust, however, that the reader is free of these dangers by now! But even with perfectly sound ideas of nature and person, it is still possible to adopt one of two different standpoints, that of the school of Antioch, or that of the school of Alexandria. He who adopts the real or existential standpoint of the unity of Christ's natures in the Person of the Word, and the actual (moral) unity of Christ's activities as God and as man, will be thinking like the Alexandrians, and must beware of the danger of confusing or commingling his two activities into one. On the other hand, he who begins by considering the activities of Christ in his human nature must avoid the besetting sin of the Antiocheans, and not allow himself to be betrayed into attributing an independence to Christ's human will it never had, for this just prepares the way for regarding the actions of Christ in his human nature as the actions of a mere man different from those of the Word himself. We have

[4] St Thomas, *Summa Theologica*, III, qu. 19, art 1.

seen that the Faith requires that we should hold firmly to both truths, firstly, that the Person of Christ is that of the Word of God, and secondly that the Word of God, without ceasing to be divine in his nature, took to himself a human nature. Thus the one Person of the Word Incarnate has two distinct activities, one divine and one human. Furthermore, in order to give a complete account of Christ's activities we must look beyond the activities themselves to their end, their intended effect, that of our redemption from sin.

In choosing the line he would follow St Thomas made use of two principles which he accepted as metaphysically necessary, and which he linked together with the aid of the principle of causality. The first of these principles we have already mentioned in connection with the doctrine of the hypostatic union: *actiones sunt suppositorum*, actions belong to persons. The second is: *Operari sequitur esse*, activity comes from, and according to being. He studied the activity of Christ with the aid of these metaphysical principles, conjoined with his doctrine of instrumental causality applied to his human nature as the instrument conjoined to the divinity, and thus developed the theological approach of the school of Alexandria. As we have seen, this human nature, conjoined though it be to the Word, preserves its own proper nature, and the distinctive characteristics of its own activity, just as the Word Incarnate, in the activities which are properly divine and common to the three divine Persons, preserves the properties and activities of the divine nature. In explaining the rules for the Communication of Idioms we have seen how it is that the properties of the two natures in Christ are not interchangeable. The same conditions of non-interchangeableness necessarily apply to the operations of the natures in Christ, and (of course) we have to adhere rigidly to the law that "the plurality of activities does not prejudice the unity of Christ's Person".[5] But if there are two kinds of activity in Christ, even as there are two natures, and if we must insist that, as the Word of God, Christ acted

[5] St Thomas, *Summa Theologica*, III, qu. 19, art 1 ad 4.

divinely through his divine nature without his human nature having any share in such activity (thus, as God, Christ maintains the world in existence and is present everywhere), and humanly through his human nature and will, the activities of his human nature which subsists in the Person of the Word depend entirely on the Person of the Word to whom alone they ultimately belong, and to whom alone they owe their existence. There is no duality of origin in Christ's activities, some belonging to the Word, and some not belonging to the Word.

All his human activities are *theandric* in some sense of the term, either because they are operations of the Word himself in which the human nature works dependently on the divine nature as its instrument, as, for example, in the case of Christ's miracles and prophecies (these are theandric acts in the strict sense of the term), or because they are the operations of the Word himself in his human nature, as, for example, are the daily actions of Christ as man (these can be called theandric acts in the wide sense of the term). The Word of God raised Lazarus from the tomb, and the Word of God wept because Lazarus was dead; the Word of God prophesied that Peter would deny him three times, and the Word of God washed Peter's feet. A duality of origin in his activities would inevitably lead to a theory of duality of persons in Christ. As Fr de Montcheuil wrote:

> The human actions of Christ are the actions of the Word of God. To admit a human person in Christ would be tantamount to saying that his actions are those of a man inspired by God, united to God as closely as one could conceive, but still not the actions of God. The life of Jesus Christ would then be that of a representative of God on earth, surpassing in dignity and perfection the activities of all those who might have gone before him: but it would not be the very life of God himself on earth.[6]

Something of the wondrous riches of the doctrine of the hypostatic union now comes vividly before the mind. The strict

[6] Y. de Montcheuil, *Leçons sur le Christ*, pp. 54–5.

theandric actions of Christ show us the Word using his human will at the service of his divine will. The moment at which Christ performed a theandric action, he performed numerically *one* act, and the Person of the Word would claim it in its totality as his own for he alone was the author of the act, but this one act was both divine and human. Thus Jesus could say that his works, his miracles and prophecies, witnessed to his being the Son of God, for such actions bore the imprint of divine agency as plainly as the act of creation itself. His contemporaries, those at least who were not blind, realized that Christ was indeed not the mere man he at first appeared to them to be: "Why, who is this, who gives his command to wind and water, and is obeyed?" (Luke 8. 25: Mark 4. 41). "Never did man speak as this man" (Matt. 13. 27). Expressions like these, of which there are many in the Gospels, show that those who knew Christ, and beheld the deeds he performed in his human nature, realized that he was not just human. They realized that his human nature lay mysteriously but firmly rooted in a Person who was so far above anything human as to be divine.

Christ's human activities were theandric activities, for though human in outward manifestation, they were divine in origin, power and nature or character: while on earth the Word of God used his human nature as an instrument, and an instrument that was so much his own as to be conjoined to his divine Person. Thus he manifested his divinity in and through his human nature. The theandric activity of Christ must not be thought of "as a synthetic activity", in which the human operation is in some way absorbed in the divine, but as the use that Christ made of his natural human powers, as instruments directed by his divine powers, to produce effects that were divine in character. Thus Christ's act of healing a leper was one action: it was the work of his human nature in so far as Christ the Word used his body to touch and speak to the sick man, but the work of his human nature was conjointly and inseparably one with that divine activity of the Word who was the principal cause of the cure, for it was God who assured to the physical touch and the human word the superhuman efficacy which was purely divine.[7]

The theandric activities of Christ belong to him to the exclusion of the other Persons of the Blessed Trinity. The Word of God alone worked our redemption by dying on the cross, and thus the Creed says that the Son of God was born and suffered for us. The Father and the Holy Spirit had no part in this work, though they expressed together as God their love for mankind in willing the Incarnation and our Redemption. The exact statement of the Creed that Christ alone suffered for our sins avoids all the false theories of the Patripassians who considered that the Father himself suffered in Christ's passion. God died on the cross, but solely in so far as he was a man, and as only the Person of the Word became a man, only the Person of the Word died on the cross.

The purely human actions, such as eating, sleeping, walking, growing, etc., of Christ were truly those of the man Jesus Christ, but as Christ the man is the divine Person of the Word, these actions were also divine by reason of their being the acts of a divine Person. These actions can be called theandric in a wide sense of the term, for they were not intrinsically dependent on the divine power or the divine nature for being performed. But they are theandric in the sense that they, too, as the acts of the Word working to redeem men, contributed towards their salvation. When Jesus walked, he performed an action which is specifically human in character, but it contributed towards our redemption which was a work specifically divine in character. Similarly when our Lord was baptized he performed purely human actions, but it was an important act in the programme of his public ministry. When Jesus suffered and died on the cross he suffered and died in his human nature alone, but this physical, bodily death saved all men, and his bodily resurrection assures us all of salvation. Both the death and resurrection of Christ were theandric actions, the resurrec-

[7] St Thomas, *Summa Theologica*, iii, qu. 18, art. 1; and qu. 19, art. 1.

tion in the strict, and the death in the wide sense of the term.

Christian piety has always been nourished by the contemplation of Christ's human activities, and the Church gives expression to her contemplation of them in her prayers and liturgy. The whole liturgy of the Eucharist is, in a special way, expressive of the doctrine of the Word Incarnate. The Body of Christ, formed in the womb of the Virgin Mary by the power of the Holy Spirit, and which we adore in the Sacrament of the Altar, is present on the Altar to impart to us Christ's own virtues. The Eucharist "guards our souls unto eternal life", and "frees us from the effects of sin", and reception of the Eucharist in Holy Communion accomplishes our salvation *now*. A glance at a few of the numerous Postcommunion prayers in the Missal will be enough to reveal how the Church would have us pray with the thought of the actions of the Incarnate Word ever in our minds. The petitions in these prayers are only explicable in terms of the doctrine we have outlined of Christ's theandric activity. On numerous occasions we must have recited the prayer of St Ignatius Loyola: "Soul of Christ sanctify me. Body of Christ save me. Blood of Christ inebriate me. . . ." No utterance of personal devotion expresses so eloquently the doctrine imparted to us by the most rigorous theological thinking!

THE KNOWLEDGE OF CHRIST

As we have seen, the Third Council of Constantinople defined as a truth of faith the existence in Christ of two activities (*operationes*): hence it is necessary to recognize in him two sources and kinds of knowledge, just as we recognize two different wills. The basic importance of the part played by knowledge in all human activity, and indeed the importance of knowledge itself as one of the noblest of all human activities, goes without saying; naturally enough it was a favourite theme in the writings of St Thomas. From the point of view of methodology, then, it is quite natural to pass from considering the twofold activity in Christ to consider his two ways of knowing, as God and as man. As God, Christ possessed the divine knowledge of God proper to each of the Persons of the Trinity; and as man he also possessed human knowledge and the human way of knowing common to all men. The divine knowledge of Christ was the uncreated knowledge of the Word, equal to that of the Father and Holy Spirit: by this knowledge Christ knew God in himself and all other beings in God. Christ's human knowledge was entitatively different from this divine knowledge, for his human knowledge was possessed by his human and not his divine mind. Theologians further distinguish various forms of knowledge in Christ's human mind:

(a) From the first moment of his conception Christ's human soul enjoyed the beatific vision of the Godhead. This knowledge belonged to his human soul by right of the hypostatic union; thus Christ had a human knowledge of his divine Being and Personality and he always had in the highest possible intensity this knowledge that the Saints enjoy in heaven.

(b) Christ's human mind was also endowed with infused knowledge analogous to that of the angels, that is to say, he had the knowledge created spirits are granted by God of all that is equal to them and inferior to them in being, and some knowledge about God himself more perfect than any which man has by nature.

(c) As a man like in all things to us Christ had also an acquired and a truly empirical knowledge which he gained from his contact with men and earthly realities during his life on earth.

This way of considering Christ's knowledge, with all its divisions and distinctions, may well appear to be due to a purely analytical way of thinking about Christ and to involve a sort of atomization of his Personality; it looks perhaps as though we are being asked to adopt the artificial process of thrusting upon a living person a number of purely logical, academical classifications only to find ourselves confronted at the end with the puzzle of having to fit them together into a unity. It is, however, very important for the reader to realize once and for all that the psychology of Christ has to be studied by the theologian in an analytical manner as this is the only way in which he can study it, and do any justice at all to what the Scriptures tell us about this knowledge. We cannot possibly hope to understand the mystery of the harmonious accord of all these different kinds of knowledge as they existed in Christ himself. We believe indeed that in Christ all the kinds of knowledge he possessed blended together into a perfect synthesis, but we have no means of knowing anything at all about Christ's own experience of his own knowledge. The different kinds of knowledge we distinguish, and which we recognize in what the Scriptures tell us about his knowledge, may well appear to split the unity of Christ's conscious life up into an apparent number of separate compartments; but we can rectify this defect in the way we have to think by stating that they did not exist like separate compartments in Christ's own knowing. One and the same Person knew both as God and as man, and there was a unity in Christ's knowing as there was in his willing, but it is more difficult for us to find a way of thinking the unity in his knowing than the unity in his willing. The reader who appreciates the extraordinary difficulties under which we are labouring in this mystery will be more tolerant of the many distinctions we have to make.

We are considering now solely the knowledge of Christ's human mind, and not that he possessed as God. First of all it is certain that Christ always enjoyed the knowledge of the beatific vision, and that he saw the divine nature as it is in itself because of the hypostatic union of his human nature with the Person of the Word. But mindful as ever of the principle that the hypostatic union did not in any way impair the natural life of his human nature, we must deny any suggestion that the enjoyment of the beatific vision suppressed or minimized the purely natural activities of his human mind. Christ also' had the purely human mental and imaginative life which all men enjoy. As God, Christ knew all things, and as man his human mind saw all things in God; if, however, his human mind never had a human way of knowing things as well, Christ could not have lived as a real man and his human mind would never have experienced the natural activity of thinking on its own. If he had never used his human mind naturally in a purely human kind of way, he would not have been like other men in his inner life and experience. As we must insist on the genuine reality of his human life, we must obviously insist that Christ used his human mind in a purely human way, that he needed to, and did acquire a knowledge about people and things like other men, and that he developed powers of reasoning as all men do. Thus Christ certainly showed himself on many occasions to be highly skilled and quick in argument, and more than a match for the subtlest of his enemies (see Matt. 12. 2–8; 21. 23–28; 22. 15–22; John, 7. 45–47; 8. 1–11). Knowledge belongs to a person by reason of his nature, and thus a real difference of natures shows that Christ necessarily had both a purely divine and a purely human way of knowing. As no purely human act of knowledge can ever know the hypostatic union, Christ's purely human knowledge could not have been a knowledge resulting from that union.

A decree of the Holy Office issued on June 5th, 1918, declared that the three following propositions could not safely be taught:

(i) It is not established that the soul of Christ, while he was living among men, had the beatific vision.

(ii) It is not certain that the soul of Christ was not ignorant of anything, but knew from the beginning all things in the Word, that is, things past, present and future, or all that God knows by the knowledge of vision.

(iii) The thesis of certain modern theologians about the limited knowledge of Christ's soul has as rightful a place in the Catholic schools as the teaching of older theologians concerning his universal knowledge.[8]

[8] See Denzinger, 2183–5.

This document marks out clearly what must be taught and what the Church has left to the free discussions of theologians.[9] It is of faith that Christ had a truly human knowledge and that ignorance cannot be a weakness of mind attributable to him. St Augustine has given us the reason for this: as ignorance resembles concupiscence in being a source of sin, it can have no place in Christ's soul. The beatific vision, granted to his soul as a grace with the hypostatic union, is the source of Christ's knowledge of all things. The acquisition of knowledge by empirical means had a place in Christ's life, not because he needed to acquire knowledge he did not possess at all, but simply because he was a man and had a man's need for knowledge acquired by experience in addition to any other kind of knowledge he possessed. We cannot possibly subscribe to the old Docetist error and imagine that Christ only feigned to learn and know like other men. The Church leaves theologians free to discuss the nature both of his acquired and of his infused knowledge, Scripture being less explicit about them than about Christ's divine knowledge.

THE KNOWLEDGE OF THE BEATIFIC VISION

From the first moment of his conception, Christ's human mind perceived God himself, and he was aware of the mission with which he as the Word was entrusted by the Father. "My testimony is trustworthy, even when I testify on my own behalf; I know whence I have come, and where I am going" (John 8. 14). Christ could not have been ignorant even for a single moment of the prerogatives and attributes of God because the hypostatic union put his mind in a closer union with God than

---

[9] The reader should bear in mind that a document of this kind issued by the Holy Office is not intended to imply that the contradictory of the propositions stated are truths of faith. It only implies that these propositions as they stand are not to be taught or defended as true by theologians because there is no sufficient evidence to show that they are true. Such a decree could be revoked at any time should the Holy Office consider that the reasons which rendered its promulgation necessary or prudent in 1918 no longer hold.

any created mind will ever be even in heaven. To those who say that Christ only became conscious of his divine nature gradually as time passed, we need only reply that the episode of the finding in the Temple related by St Luke shows Christ's human awareness of God the Father as clearly as any of his later statements recorded by St John, such as "Before ever Abraham came to be, I am". Jesus replied to his Mother's expression of anxiety at having lost him: "What reason had you to search for me? Could you not tell that I must needs be in the place which belongs to my Father?" (Luke 2. 49). Fr Lagrange comments on the words, ἐν τοῖς τοῦ πατρός μου δεῖ εἶναι με, as follows: "St Luke intended that we should understand how Jesus, at the age of twelve, had a clear understanding of his divine origin. The evangelist does not attribute this knowledge he had to a revelation, nor to a progressive realization. He had this knowledge from that unique, immediate intellectual vision which alone was such as to enable his mind to behold the distinction of Father, Son and Spirit in the ineffable Trinity itself."[10]

One difficulty, however, arises immediately about the universality of Christ's knowledge, and it is, of course, the one which the Arians raised of old: what are we to say about Christ's professed ignorance of the day of judgement? St Mark records our Lord's own words: "But as for that day and that hour you speak of, they are known to nobody, not even to the angels in heaven, not even to the Son: only the Father knows them" (Mark 13. 32). Biblical exegetes have struggled manfully with this difficult text. Certain modern Rationalists, as, for example, Loisy, have questioned its authenticity. This, however, is the one thing about the text that seems quite unquestionable. Fr Lagrange has summarized the theological problem it presents as follows:

The Arians used this verse to show the absolute inferiority of the Son to the Father. The Fathers rebutted their arguments

[10] M. L. Lagrange, *The Gospel of Jesus Christ*, I, p. 51.

by saying either that Jesus spoke here purely as man, and solely of what he knew as a man, or by casting doubts on the authenticity of the text, or by unduly forcing it in the way that St Basil tried to do: the Son, he said, was said by Christ not to know the day of judgement, if the Father did not know it, for the knowledge of the Son is derived as from its source, from that of the Father. The text is, however, undoubtedly authentic and must be accepted as such, and it does not treat of the purely human knowledge of the Saviour, or of what he knew purely as a man. Some of the Fathers and many theologians have tried to solve the problem by making another distinction: the Son knew the day of judgement, but he had not the authority to impart what for lack of such authority "he did not know" in the sense that "he was not sent by the Father to reveal or make known". This distinction may appear perhaps too subtle, and too much like a loophole device for those bent on an escape at any cost. It is nonetheless perfectly sound as a solution, and clearly recognizable as such, so long as one remembers that the term Father denotes God as inaccessible to, and hidden from men's minds. The Father reveals divine truths to men by the Son, and he also communicates with men by the ministry of his angels. Whatever does not form a part of the message which either the Son or the angels have authority to impart to men, must remain absolutely secret. In brief, if we distinguish the Son from the Father formally, saying that the Son is the Son as sent by the Father to men, Christ is saying that he has not the competent authority to manifest this secret knowledge.[11]

In addition to the knowledge of his divine mission Christ also had the knowledge of all things in God which the saints in heaven enjoy. As Pius XII wrote in his encyclical *Mystici Corporis*, commenting on the words of St Paul in the Epistle to the Colossians 1. 19: "He also enjoys the beatific vision (*scientia visionis*) in a degree, both as regards extent and clarity, surpassing that of all the saints in heaven" (sect. 46). This knowledge of all things in God is a permanent endowment of Christ's human nature: he was never without it, even

[11] See M. J. Lagrange, *L'Évangile de Saint Marc*, third edition, pp. 326–7.

in his sufferings on the cross. In his final abandonment before death Jesus preserved unimpaired in the depths of his soul the vision of God. This should not cause us any surprise. After all do we not often preserve, in our own human sufferings and afflictions, a very delicate and intense realization of the value of suffering? And is not this realization a source of strength to us which fortifies us against the possibility of even greater moral or physical suffering than we have yet endured? The lives of the great martyrs show that a man's acceptance of suffering can even become more resolute as the suffering continues, and leave his soul in peace. Theologians have often used a purely physical example to help us see something of the mystery of the imperturbable depths of Jesus' human soul on the cross:

> A storm can lash the sides of a mountain, and let loose on it rain, hail, and lightning. But nothing disturbs the peace of the mountain heights. They remain calm and serene amidst the furore. The snow-capped mountain tops continue to shine beneath the rays of the sun above. Thus it was with the soul of Jesus: he enjoyed light and joy from the vision of God in the highest point of his soul hidden from our gaze, though outwardly he was a man afflicted by all manner of evils and pains, sin and ignorance alone excepted.[12]

INFUSED KNOWLEDGE

This particular kind of knowledge belongs by nature, as we have said, to the angels. Their own distinctive kind of intellectual activity is based on ideas which God infused into their minds at their creation. Christ also must have been endowed with this superhuman kind of knowledge: this is, at least, the opinion of all Catholic theologians and it is based on the teaching of Scripture about the universal sovereignty of Christ over all creatures, and in particular about his sovereignty over all the angels. By the knowledge of the beatific vision Christ saw all things in God and as related to God; by his infused know-

[12] M. Vigué, *Le Christ*, p. 471.

ledge he knew all kinds of secrets, hidden from men and even the angels, about created things themselves. The Church has never defined that Christ did in fact have this innate knowledge which theologians attribute to him; theological conclusions are not necessarily revealed truths, even if they are of importance in theology. On this particular point of Christ's infused knowledge St Thomas and St Bonaventure are in agreement in all but words, St Thomas being, it seems, more definite in what he says than St Bonaventure. The characteristic of this kind of knowledge is that it is entirely spiritual, being independent of experience. Though our Lord's infused knowledge would have been more extensive than that of any of the angels, his human mind did not always advert to all that it knew, and at any one moment of his human life this knowledge must have been, as we say, latent within his mind and available for use when needed.

It is after all perfectly natural for the human mind to have knowledge both in the sense that something is actually known and adverted to here and now, and in the sense that we are able to think about it and understand it at will. By comparison with the knowledge of the angels, however, Christ's infused knowledge was less perfect in one sense, viz., that as angelic knowledge is knowledge by purely spiritual minds, and as pure spirits are free from the limitations of matter, their power of intellectual vision and synthesis is far greater than that of any human mind which is up to a point dependent on the body. But the actual understanding that the Word gave to Christ's human mind would have more than compensated for this natural incompleteness in his infused knowledge at any one moment of his life and thus the intensity and depth of his human understanding during the whole course of his life would have been far greater than any in the angelic world. As Fr Vigué says pointedly: "there would have been many more acts of thinking on Christ's part than on the part of an angel, but Christ would have had greater infused knowledge and understood more in the multiplicity of his mental acts."[13]

[13] M. Vigué, *op. cit.*, p. 475.

ACQUIRED OR EMPIRICAL KNOWLEDGE

The mind of man acquires knowledge from the senses, and as a true man Christ must have used his mind together with his senses to acquire a knowledge of the world of things and people around him by ordinary human means. There must have been some way in which Christ could genuinely acquire a knowledge of the people and things of this world, and some sense in which we can say that, though he knew them super-humanly, he nonetheless knew them humanly as well, that is to say by a knowledge coming from sensation and experience. Jesus "grew and came to strength", and he "advanced in wisdom with the years" (Luke 2. 40, 52), and the growth, both physical and mental, was really that of a child. We must adhere firmly to this position to avoid the dangers of Docetism.

Furthermore, if Christ's human knowledge was really, and not just apparently, human there must have been some limits to the knowledge he could have acquired by means of his senses and human experience. Today we have very different ideas about the limitations of a man's capacities for acquiring knowledge than anyone had during the Middle Ages, and we may perhaps be not a little surprised at St Thomas' ideas of the extent of Christ's purely human and acquired knowledge. In his early *Commentary on the Sentences* of Peter Lombard he held that the mind of Christ, perfect from the first moment of its existence, cannot have been at any time in a purely poten-tial state of complete nescience, so that it could not have had an intrinsic need of being aroused to activity by contact with material realities. During the years between his commenting on the *Sentences* and writing the third Part of the *Summa Theo-logica*, his thought developed considerably on most of the basic problems of Christology, largely as a result of his study of the Greek Fathers during his years in Italy. But his ideas about the extent of Christ's human knowledge never underwent any noticeable change. When he wrote the *Summa Theologica*, however, he was alive to the necessity of insisting on the full reality of Christ's human nature and all its natural activities, and he certainly emphasized the reality of the experimental qualities of his knowledge as a man.

Nonetheless, the undeveloped ideas of those times concerning man's ways of acquiring a knowledge of the physical world, together with his awareness of the absolute pre-eminence of Christ as a man over all created beings, led the Angelic Doctor to attribute a vastness of knowledge to Christ in his purely human ways of knowing which nothing in the Scriptures indicates that he possessed. He argued that the perfection of Christ's acquired knowledge must have been such as to have befitted his mission, and no doubt our Lord did set himself to acquire such knowledge no matter how extensive that may have been. One modern writer, Mgr Chollet, has really said as much as it is humanly possible for us to say:

The knowledge which we have nowadays from the sciences was possessed by Christ by infused knowledge: he was certainly not ignorant of what we call the secrets of nature. But we must recognize that Christ had no wish to set himself forward as, nor to acquire the reputation of being, a learned chemist or physicist, nor a skilful doctor. He had other preoccupations and a higher vocation for which to live. Consequently, his experience of the physical world was not that of the scientific experimenter looking for data; he did not examine the stars as an astronomer, nor the plants as a botanist, nor the elements as a chemist, nor man as an anatomist. He left all such human activities and interests severely alone, and devoted himself to a higher point of view so far as material things were concerned in his life. He thought of things as forming a harmonious whole or universe, and as dependent on their Creator. He listened for the voice which speaks to reason of all things as related to God, and which raises the mind beyond them to God in a hymn of praise and thanksgiving. He looked for the action of God's providence within the world. A supernatural psychologist, he sounded souls, their wounds and the profound transformations worked in them by divine grace. His ever watchful and observant mind sought God in the universe and in men's lives, God's reflection in creatures, the use of created things for the good of souls, and the orienta-

tion of souls to their supreme end, namely the love and possession of God. Hence the Gospels use an apter word to convey
their meaning than "science": St Luke tells us that Jesus grew
in wisdom, that is, that higher life of the spirit which is absorbed
with the thought about the divine importance of all things, and
problems about the destiny and the mystery of what lies beyond
time in eternity.[14]

These words of Mgr Chollet call for no lengthy comment:
so long as we keep to the key principle that Christ had a perfectly natural human mind, nothing further need be said. Each
theologian can add what he sees fit for himself according to his
own ideas of what human knowledge is and involves. During
the Middle Ages men shared a certain Platonic ideal of human
knowledge which they conceived as being acquired purely and
simply by the use of the mind and its insight into the essences
of objects presented in experience. Nowadays we find such a
conception of human knowledge difficult even to envisage, and
it would be foolhardy to claim for Christ, who deigned to live
in a backward part of Galilee, an acquired scientific knowledge of the world, the use of which would not in any case have
contributed to the work of redeeming men from sin. This kind
of purely "human ignorance" in Christ could not be an effect
of sin, nor have involved him in any leaning towards error
or sin. It is most wise to subscribe to the genial idea of Pascal:
"Jesus Christ, without wealth, and without any outward show
of science, is in his own order of sanctity. He never made in-
ventions, and he never reigned; but he was humble, patient,
holy, holy to God, terrible to demons, and without sin. But,
how great is the splendour and how amazing the magnificence
in which he has come to the eyes of those who cherish
wisdom."[15]

[14] See M. Vigué, *op. cit.*, p. 478.
[15] Pascal, *Pensées*, 793.

SELECT BIBLIOGRAPHY

In this series: CHENU, M. D., O.P.: *Is Theology a Science?*; CRISTIANI, Léon: *Heresies and Heretics*; PIAULT, Bernard: *What is the Trinity?*; RONDET, Henri, S.J.: *Do Dogmas Change?*

ADAM, Karl: *Christ our Brother*, London and New York, Sheed and Ward, 1931; *The Son of God*, London and New York, Sheed and Ward, 1934; *The Christ of Faith*, London, Burns and Oates, and New York, Pantheon, 1957.

ARENDZEN, J. P.: *Whom do you say—?*, London, Sands, 1927.

ATHANASIUS, St: *The Incarnation of the Word of God*, translated by a Religious of C.S.M.V., London, Centenary Press, and New York, Macmillan, 1944.

AUGUSTINE, St: *Enchiridion*, translated by Marcus Dods, Edinburgh, Clark, 1873; *On St John's Gospel*, translated by John Gibb, Edinburgh, Clark, 1873.

CERFAUX, F.: *Christ in the Theology of St Paul*, London and New York, Nelson, 1960.

DENZINGER-BANNWART: *Enchiridion Symbolorum*, thirty-first edition by Umberg-Rahner, Freiburg, Herder, 1960.

FELDER, H.: *Christ and the Critics*, two volumes, London, Burns and Oates, 1924; *Jesus of Nazareth*, Milwaukee, Bruce, 1953.

FORTESCUE, A.: *The Greek Fathers*, London, Catholic Truth Society, 1908.

GRAHAM, A., O.S.B.: *The Christ of Catholicism*, London and New York, Longmans, 1947.

GRANDMAISON, L. de, S.J.: *Jesus Christ*, three volumes, London and New York, Sheed and Ward, 1935.

HÉRIS, C. V., O.P.: *The Mystery of Christ*, Cork, Mercier Press, 1950.

HUGHES, P.: *History of the Church*, volume I, London and New York, Sheed and Ward, 1947.

IGNATIUS of Antioch, St: *Epistles*, translated by J. A. Kleist, London, Longmans, and Westminster, Md, Newman Press, 1946.

LAGRANGE, M. J., O.P.: *The Gospel of Jesus Christ*, London, Burns and Oates, 1938, and Westminster, Md, Newman Press, 1943.

LATTEY, C., S.J. (editor): *The Incarnation* (Cambridge Summer School Lectures), Cambridge, Heffer, 1926.

LEO, St: *Select Sermons on the Incarnation*, translated by W. Bright, London, Masters, 1886.

McKENZIE, J. L., S.J.: *The Two-Edged Sword*, London, Geoffrey Chapman, 1960.

MAURIAC, F.: *Life of Jesus*, New York, McKay, 1951.

NEWMAN, J. H.: *Parochial and Plain Sermons*, London, Rivingtons, 1875; *Lectures on Justification*, London, Rivingtons, 1874.

PRAT, F., S.J.: *The Theology of St Paul*, two volumes, London, Burns and Oates, 1938, and Westminster, Md, Newman Press, 1958.

VONIER, A., O.S.B.: *The Personality of Christ* and *The Victory of Christ* reprinted in *The Collected Works*, London, Burns and Oates, and Westminster, Md, Newman Press, 1952.

A Catholic Commentary on Holy Scripture, London and New York, Nelson, 1953.

The Twentieth Century Encyclopedia of Catholicism

The number of each volume indicates its place in the over-all series and not the order of publication.

TWENTIETH CENTURY ENCYCLOPEDIA OF CATHOLICISM

All titles are subject to change.